The Writers' Wives

The Writers' Wives

CONTRA COSTA COUNTY LIBRARY

Edited by
Narita M. Gonzalez

Anvil

The Writers' Wives
Edited by Narita M. Gonzalez

Copyright of the anthology © NARITA M. GONZALEZ
and ANVIL PUBLISHING, INC., 2000

Copyright of the essays remains with their respective authors.

All rights reserved.
No part of this book may be reproduced
in any form or by any means
without the written permission
of the copyright owners.

Published and exclusively distributed by
ANVIL PUBLISHING, INC.
2/F Team Pacific Bldg.
P. Antonio St., Barrio Ugong
Pasig City 1604, Philippines
Telephones: 671.1899, 671.9230 (sales & marketing)
Fax: 671.9235
EMail: pubdept@anvil.com.ph

All photographs provided by the authors.

Cover photograph of Rebecca and Agapito Gaddi by June Poticar Dalisay
Cover design by June Poticar Dalisay
Interior design by Gerry R. Baclagon of Word House

ISBN 971-27-0927-2

Printed in the Philippines
by Capitol Publishing House, Inc.

To

My parents
Anselma and Cornilio Manuel, Sr.

and to

N.V.M., Ibarra, Selma, Myke and Lakshmi

Mr. Pen and Mrs. Pen-pal ?
Nick Joaquin

Ancient is the mystery this anthology of true confessions would clarify: what is the role played by a writer's spouse in the writer's office?

An immediate answer would be that the spouse is a kind of live-in pen-pal: inspiring and spurring, even speeding, the writer's pen. But on second thought this idea of the writer's spouse as the writer's muse offends by seeming to be more hackneyed sentiment than homely sense. And what hops next to the mind is Shakespear's wife, who is generally believed to have had no role at all the mill of his fancy. She was simply the wife of the would-be gentleman of Stratford but never of the poet of London. She was a pencil but not his pen, much less his pen-pal. In his will he left her the "second-best bed."

This question on the role of the writer's spouse can be brought more down to earth by juxtaposing it with a more prosaic query. For example: what is the role played by the policeman's spouse in the police station? Or: what is the role played by the butcher's spouse in the slaughterhouse? The answer is obvious: in both cases the spouse has no place at all unless also a qualified cop or butcher.

This view that a writer's spouse too can have a place in a writer's office only as meddler is the snicker in one author's dedication:

"To my darling wife, without whose unfailing help and advice this book would have been finished in half the time."

But others can object that the proper juxtaposition to the question in question is not one more prosaic but rather another on art. For instance: what is the role played by an artist's spouse in the artist's studio? And what springs to mind is Picasso, whose various spouses were his raw material; pre-palette paint waiting to be canvassed.

The parallels with certain literary spouses are evident. Virginia, the child-wife of Poe, was in life but even more in death the womb from which he extorted a poetry at once vernal and morbid, grotesque and exquisite, innocent and depraved. As wife-obsessed, though less monstrously, was James Joyce, whose epic eyes seem to have been blinded by unceasing images of his Nora, dazzling in lustful disarray. And from the German Frieda was D.H. Lawrence born again, transformed from a coalminer's offspring into a heathen high priest, a phallic mystic championing blood over mind. What Frieda bore was Lawrence the apocalypse, saying blood and genitals are the true consciousness, not intellect and thought. I come, therefore I am.

Harmonious may hardly seem the world for marriage like these: so darkly submerging and yet so loftily fruiting. But harmony, height and light, are indeed the elements of these literary union. However, there are other such matches that as recklessly plunge underground but are not always successful in coming up for air. Most notorious of all is the tragedy of Zelda and Scott Fitzgerald. If ever a match looked as if made in heaven it was this pairing of the "crown Prince and Princess of American Letters." Both had charm, beauty, vitality and vivacity. He had genius, she had talent, and they were as much in love with writing as with each other. And even more crazily in love with fame, which had kissed them early. Each should have been but a natural and welcome influence on the other. What they developed into natural and welcome influence on the other. But they developed into was each other's destruction. She went mad, he cracked up.

What made both of them fatal as writer's spouse?

Hemingway said that Zelda was jealous of Scott's genius and tried to pull him down, cage him in spirit, deprive him of self-confidence. But it seems that Scott himself was envious of Zelda's writing talent and tried to stop her from using what he considered his own special material: jazz-era youth, American expatriates in Europe, the rich who are not like you and me. And he exploited Zelda spiritually, drawing on her memories to furnish his fiction. In his novel about a girl going mad he actually used letters that Zelda had written when she was going mad. A counterpoint to that would be the claim that Zelda had tried to give him an inferiority complex by telling him he was inadequately equipped sexually. (He was reassured, however, by Hemingway, after a urinal display.)

Such horror stories cannot but make us glad of our own Filipino literary marriages. These native unions seem so utterly felicitous even when the pen is both man and wife, as was the case with Manuel and Lydia Arguilla. Absent are the mutual envy and jealousy that ravaged the Fitzgeralds; a flame instead is pride in each other's gifts that impelled Lydia, long after Manuel was dead, to keep on publishing prose items "by Manuel & Lydia Arguilla." As firm an equipose kept the marriage of Ed and Edith Tiempo from see-sawing through a lifetime of debates in literary circles as to who was the genuine writer. And if ever Pete Lacaba and Marra Lanot should bicker, it wouldn't be over each other's punctuation or paragraphing. He respects her semi-colons and she likes his parentheses.

Why does the Filipino writer make—or seem to make—so equable a spouse? Is it because the Filipino, even as writer—even as genius—still is first the clansman of a barangay, bound by tribal traditions on matrimony, family, home? Thou shalt not spoil the land with as broken bed. Or is the explanation the national character—a character, 'tis said, whose first instinct is to please?

Whatever the moral, it remains true that the literary marriage, so wild a scene in other cultures, appears to be idyllic in ours. Here, the spouse, if unliterary, will make up for it with understanding—unlike Edith Wharton's golden Philistine of a husband, who saw no value in her work. Here, if the pen be erratic, the spouse can be depended on as guide—like Virginia Woolf's priceless manager of a mate, who helped her make it through the night, or others similarly as serviceable as you will read of in this book.

This is quite a historic volume: a behind-the-scenes look at our literature. Culture is always a parlor thing but here it's bedroom, bath and kitchen. Afterwards you'll be reading the author's ambushed here with 3-D specs and a smiling mind.

Happy reading!

Editor's Note

What would I find, while looking for some unpublished children's stories in an old Manila envelops but a thin magazine folded in half. It was *Woman and Home*, a Thursday supplement of *Manila Chronicle*. The editor then was Rosalinda Orosa. She had started a series on the "pains and pleasures" women experience as wives of professionals. Are there differences in lifestyle when you are married to a lawyer, a doctor, businessman or a banker? Was it an afterthought when Orosa added how was it being married to an artist or a writer? It was my piece, " My Husband is a Writer," that had started the series. This was in 1953; I had been only eleven years married to N.V.M. at this time.

"A wife must subordinate herself to her husband's world of letters!" said the heading for my article.

So nothing has changed, in so far as I was concerned, I told myself.

But how has it been for all the others—over the years? Have we fared creditably enough in the "home management" department, in writer-husband nurturance?

I made a list of names I would send copies of my article for comments. I would compile their responses, I told them. They'd all be in a book to be called *Writer's Wives and their Mistresses*.

This is the genesis of the pages that follow.

Sorry, guys. The mistresses here are not those beguiling, younger women you might fantasize about. Rather, they are the urges that men have to put words on paper so as to come up with *that* poem, *that* story, *that* essay, or *that* novel, or play, or TV or movie script.

Ah, but feminists will not like this, especially with that notion of subordination, commented Jimmy Abad. His wife Mercy has joined us in this book.

But wasn't I the first feminist in my crowd? This was before NOW—National Organization for Women—was organized. I used my maiden name for my stories and articles then. This was in the fifties. Does that seem too long ago? Those who knew I was married to N.V.M. asked, "Is Narita *already* separated?"

After a trip to Southeast Asia with my husband, I published "Women Writers of India," of which Dr. Charles Fahs of the Rockefeller Foundation remarked, "Narita, why write about women only?"

Dr. Fahs a male chauvinist? I was almost finished with another article, "Women Writers of the East." I was unable to publish this, though. I got pregnant with our fourth child.

Many distractions common to mothers—children, household responsibilities, etc.,—drain their energies and creativity. Besides, I had started to teach school. In between came moments of peace and quiet which made possible little pieces, notes, workbooks, even a journal to edit. I do have lots of material put away in folders. They were yellowing with age!

The first wife I had discussed my book with, *WWM* I now began to call it, was Rosalina Icban Castro, whose husband Jose Luna Castro was editor of the *Manila Times* for many years. He wrote a "first" in journalism in the Philippines, a handbook in text and style for reporters.

Rosing consented without hesitation to write about her life as a writer's wife. When she learned that she had anemia and had to have blood transfusions regularly, she hurried to finish her manuscript. One day, she sent me an envelope with a note. "I am too weak to type," it said. Although ill, she managed to write with a steady hand.

She died a few months later. We lost a dear friend we have known years before the war.

The account of their early years could not have been more forthright, and I felt her daughter, Ianthe de Leon,—she teaches at U.P.—could perhaps read the article and help out in preparing a manuscript for print. As it turned out, this gave her sister and brother an opportunity to read the article also.

To his Filipino classmates at Stanford can be attributed the beginnings of Len Casper's interest in the Philippines. One of them was Amador T. Daguio. He had a Fulbright grant to London but chose to go to the Philippines instead. And what a fateful decision it turned out—for both him and Linda. We were present at their wedding in 1956.

We were able to visit with them in Boston two years ago. They have a lovely home in Saxonville, with a river for a backyard. The solitude, and the riverscape and peace—all these help Linda and Len both in their work. To date, they have written easily more than a dozen and a half books between them; doubtless, many more are coming.

One late afternoon, during a break at a book launching at U.P., a young woman with bangs and such sincerity in conveying her compliments approached me and said, "Ma'am, remember me? I was your student in 'Reading.'" I had taught language arts before I went to Home Economics teaching at the U.P. Lab School. That was more than thirty years ago. How could I remember?

But she helped me out. "I am June Poticar Dalisay."

Why, of course! Wife to one of our best writers, and a much-awarded fictionist. And June (Beng to friends) now a dedicated artist.

Recently, she had a one-woman show at Ayala Museum. The fact is, June is a person of many talents. She is a conservator—a preserver of documents, paintings and the like. An accupuncturist, she has her own set of needles. She's a book designer as well, with over ten titles to her credit at this writing, including N.V.M.'s latest book *Work on the Mountain*. She agreed to do the design for *WW*.

When I mentioned to Jimmy Abad the names of the writers in my list he said I must not miss Rose Marie Bautista. Her husband is a professor at De La Salle University, a poet, a columnist, and Rose Marie's best friend.

Rose Marie and Cirilo met in Baguio, where both had been teaching at St. Louis University. Rose Marie had read some of Cirilo's poems and had thought them interesting. The poet and the teacher became good friends. But when Cirilo told Rose Marie that he loved her, she was speechless (her own words). "There goes a beautiful friendship," she said to herself.

Just about everybody—parents, friends, his and her *lavandera* included—thought that they didn't match. But after some thinking and realizing "that there were worse things than marrying a friend," Rose Marie changed her mind.

Cirilo is a very private person, Rose Marie says. He has his moods and tantrums but she knows how to ignore them. The children and teaching occupy her time. She has kept a "Joy Bank" which, I think, we wives may well have, each of us, for our own.

It was at Edna Manlapaz's launching of her biography of Gloria Manalang, which Ateneo published, that Mercy Abad told me she was going home to Misamis with her family. But she would find time there to finish her piece on Jimmy Abad. And she did!

When he learned about this, Jimmy Abad was most curious. Did she include "the tale of my favorite shirt"? No, it didn't. It would make the piece too long, Mercy said.

So Jimmy told me about how on his way to work one day he saw their gardener wearing his favorite shirt. It was, indeed, the one shirt which he liked to wear just as soon as it had been washed and ironed. Now, their gardener had it on his back!

Instead of getting angry, Jimmy asked Mercy as gently as he could, "How'd you feel if I give away your favorite, old blanket—that gift of your grandfather's?"

When Mercy and Jimmy got married at the Chapel of Holy Sacrifice, at U.P., I was the one who prepared their wedding chairs and kneelers. They were active in the parish.

Julie and Alex Hufana, until their departure for America, had been our neighbors in Area One, on the campus. Alex was among the first students of N.V.M. in Creative Writing at U.P. In that group were Virginia Moreno, Elmer Ordonez, Rony V. Diaz, Raul Ingles, Andres Cristobal Cruz, the late Pacifico (Pic) Aprieto, and Maro Santaromana.

At this point in time, Alex was already with the English Department. In those days he would join N.V.M.'s fishing "trips" at the breakwaters off Luneta. In the middle of lunch—rice and broiled *bangus* which they had brought over—Alex stopped eating all of a sudden.

Clutching his throat, he exclaimed, "Thorn!"

A fishbone had stuck in his gullet.

"Alex," said N.V.M. "you are truly a poet!"

Their fishing group included Felixberto Sta. Maria and Professor Pascual Capiz. The group did not mind going to the Pasay or Quinta Market for live bait. This had to be live *swahi* shrimps, available only at those markets between four and five in the morning, if not earlier. It was only when you had this kind of bait that going out to the breakwaters was worthwhile. For good luck, you avoided meeting pregnant women stall-keepers and black cats.

Felixberto Sta. Maria could not manage slipping a hook onto a live *swahi* shrimp. Which did not keep him from becoming president of Far Eastern University years later.

And there's Odette Alcantara, who'd join the group of "fishing professors" too. To this day, she tells what she knew then: they seldom caught fish—in spite of all that fancy gear that they took along.

One boy who always went with them was our young grade schooler. There was hardly a Sunday that he did not join his Dad at the breakwaters. When, later, he joined the Jesuits. He was asked what it was that influenced his enlisting for the priesthood, it was those fishing trips, he'd say. Those dawn hours at the breakwaters, the calm of Manila Bay, the clean, cold sea breezes, and best of all, the quiet and peace sitting on a big solid rock waiting for a nibble, and, finally a tag on the line. He thought he'd rather be a fisher of men than of fish. And all this was more than forty-three years ago...

Alex has retired and, at this writing, has gone to his hometown in La Union. He and Julie had been schoolmates, he only a year ahead. They met again in the States and were married in Berkeley.

Julie sent her piece for our collection to our address in Hayward. I had thought, upon receiving it, that she might have elaborated more on their life in the States; but on second thought, I reminded myself that comes through anyway. That there is much restraint in Julie's piece. It does invite the reader to many a moment of remembrance and thought...

Connie Reynoso Angeles and I were members of the U.P. Women's Club in Manila, of which Mrs. Ursula Clemente was adviser. Mrs. Clemente is fondly remembered for having been an advocate for long engagements; hers had been a twenty-five year one! I lost contact of Connie, but Carlos Angeles and N.V.M., friends since their newspapering days, renewed ties when N.V.M. was teaching at U.C.L.A. Connie and Carlos celebrate two wedding anniversaries, one for a secret civil marriage, and another for the grand church wedding. Connie says she has always been supportive of her poet-husband, who is rather moody when he is writing. "But it is tolerable," she added.

Edna May Landicho is always busy with her teaching or her directing plays. She is probably no busier, of course, than her husband—who, besides teaching Filipino at U.P., used to write a column, and scripts, and is an actor in both TV and the movies. Edna doesn't mind doing chores that really are a husband's "prerogative." It turns out that most writers' wives attend to such matters as house repairs, plumbing problems, leaking roofs, termite infestations, paint jobs, etc., etc. It does seem that creativity diminishes with every household distraction.

But Edna likes best Doming's attitude about the noise that his children raise in the house. It doesn't bother him when they interrupt him. He continues on with whatever he is writing later.

I don't know if it was a romance of the First Quarter Storm, but was Alma becoming too fascinated by a young activist? The fascination led to marriage and then, for both of them to an exile in China.

What was life in China those days? Alma's "Peking Apples" gives us glimpses of how she and her husband managed. How she cared for a sick husband in a foreign land and her experiences of having babies away from home besides.

Has the China experience enriched their lives and their Filipinoness? And how did they find the home country on their return to the Philippines?

"Marriage is hard work but marriage to a writer is harder." All the wives in this book agree with Medy Cruz. Hers is a beautiful title, "The Wind Beneath His Wings". Her husband, though, is "opinionated," she says and who's writer-husband isn't? Two daughters who agreed on that point, said that their parents' "marriage is one of the best we have ever seen!"

Isagani is perhaps the most "romantic" husband in this book. Who would send a rose to his wife while in a car behind him? The flower boy looked bewildered, Medy says, "There's this middle-age man sending a flower to a middle-age woman out there on the street." But knowing that she's the one and only woman in his life has kept Medy young, happy and attractive.

As her name implies, Joy has been so to her friends. But more especially it must be to Tony Enriquez, who has decided to quit regular office work and devote his time to writing. Joy doesn't mind. She believes in his art. Now we wonder how much inspiration Tony draws from Joy's skill at the piano. Besides this talent, she accepts all the travelling that Tony has to make. She even joins him in those trips. She accompanies him to a lot of fishing trips. Who catches the first fish? The writer or the pianist?

Tony has a big book project, and Joy believes it's an important book that he must finish and publish.

I met Preciosa Soliven ages ago, when she wore pinafores and had curly long hair. She would come along to our U.P. Gang get-togethers with her aunt, Mrs. Elisa Quiroque Palma. In our group were Elisa Palma, Elsa Arellano (Syjuco), Meggie Shea, Beingina Gomez, Veronica Arevalo (Vinhian), Naty Pardo (de la Rama), and Rose Manalac (Jaime). Nina Estrada (Puyat) would sometimes join the group. Nina was the only writer in the group, though; she was a poet.

Then in the mid-60s, we met Preciosa again in Rome. She was on her way to Peruggia, to study Italian. She and Max Soliven were already married then. Being much younger than he, she likes being called "Commander-in-Chief" which Max does not mind because he gave her that title.

Max took a strong position against martial law, as many will remember. He was consequently picked up and imprisoned. "The power of the press" gave Max the "zeal of spreading the truth." (St. Francis de Sales)

* * *

At least of twenty wives to whom I wrote for essays about their husbands, one said she'd join but will write some other time. She expected me, she said, to write a number two book on writers' wives. Three wanted to join the project but their husbands thought it was not such a "good idea." Two wives accepted the invitation but they were always going on trips abroad. Two wives promised to write but when reminded about their manuscripts never returned calls. One was eager to write but kept asking for postponements. Finally, a deadline was set and unfortunately, she never made it.

The wives who wrote their pieces are married to poets, fictionists, journalists and literary critics. This, to the editor's knowledge, is the first time writer's wives have expressed their part in the partnership with a special group of men.

All twelve of them stand "behind" their writer-husbands and do not nag that they are not earning enough to support the family in style.

The writers have to hold other jobs to help out. The children are not neglected. So far there were no reports of delinquency from the writers' families. A great pride for all of us.

The editor ends her piece by sharing with you a prayer she found two years ago in a prayerbook. It's not a prayer for asking petitions. It's a prayer for guidance to writers.

Prayer to St. Francis de Sales, Patron Saint of Writers

Most loving and humble Saint, you preached to thousands with the pen introducing them to "devout life." You wrote sublimely about God's love *and made countless converts by your Christ-like kindness* Make writers realize the power of the Press, and inspire them with your zeal for spreading the truth. Help them to write honestly no matter what the subject, so that they will really contribute to bring about God's kingdom. (From: Patrons of Professions)

* * *

A big reward came N.V.M.'s way when he was awarded the National Artist for Literature in 1997. After many years of good health, he was found to need a brain operation before he starts dialysis because of renal failure. But keeping faith to his art, to a "devout life" of letters and writing "honestly" has been paid off by his becoming an *Artista ng Bayan*. Without the help of the National Commission on

Culture and the Arts (NCCA), N.V.M.'s life could be cut short by financial constraints. Otherwise, all's well in art and old age.

But all did not do well in art and old age for NVM.

On November 24, 1999, NVM slipped on the inside of the front entrance of the National Kidney Institute. He struck the right side of his face on the floor causing him to bite his right upper lip. A security guard got him a wheel chair. Two NKI employees and I helped him up and sat him on the wheel chair. He usually walks up by himself to go to the dialysis station on the second floor. He was hooked to his dialysis machine at 7:00 a.m. I asked the nurse to give first aid to the bleeding lip which he got because of the fall.

NVM had his snacks of hard cooked egg and grapes. We discussed the short story of Cecilia Brainhard, which NVM read in the *Graphic*. When I asked him if he wanted a sip of water around 9:30 a.m. or so, he couldn't answer. He had become unconscious. I called Pat, the nurse. The doctor on duty and the nurses couldn't revive him. His nephrologist was called. She said it was better to bring the unconscious patient to the Cardinal Santos Hospital for his nuerologist to see him. The CT Scan showed massive hemorrhage. The doctor said it was a brain stroke. The trauma of the fall had triggered the massive bleeding. NVM was now in coma. A life support system kept him alive until our children arrived from California. My daughter was able to see her Dad still alive but the boys arrived too late. NVM died on November 28, 1999 at exactly 11:50 p.m., the first Sunday of Advent.

* * *

To N from the other N
God called his name. NVM heard.
Quietly he left wife, family and friends.
If God had set him free
Let not my inconsolable grief be in the way
That I may also let him go free.

Contents

Mr. Pen—and Mrs. Pen-pal?
    NICK JOAQUIN   vii

Editor's Note   xi

MERCY RIVERA ABAD
    I Married a Poet   1

CONCEPCION REYNOSO ANGELES
    The Writer's Wife   17

ROSE MARIE J. BAUTISTA
    Joy Bank   25

LINDA TY CASPER
    Being Married to a Writer   31

ROSALINA ICBAN CASTRO
    "To My Darling Wife"   43

REMEDIOS CALMA CRUZ
    The Wind Beneath His Wings   49

JUNE POTICAR DALISAY
    The Early Years   63

JOY VIERNES ENRIQUEZ
    A Never-ending Tale   75

NARITA MANUEL GONZALEZ
Our Life on File 97

JULITA QUIMING HUFANA
Marriage Made in Heaven 119

EDNA MAY LANDICHO
Music to My Ears 137

ALMA CRUZ MICLAT
Peking Apple 145

PRECIOSA S. SOLIVEN
Commander-in-Chief 165

About the Wives 183

Mercy Rivera Abad
I Married a Poet

※✿※

From the very start, it was an unlikely match. Jimmy was a campus figure and had the pretty girls in tow, while I was one of the Engineering boys. He read stuffy books; I wielded a slide rule. I remember often seeing him surrounded by wide-eyed pretty ones; while I roughed it up with boys who knew how to cut classes, make engines run, soil their hands in the process, and play a mean game of bowling and billiards. I knew some of the girls who secretly had a crush on Jimmy; even helped one organize a *despedida* party for him before he left for the US.

As students, we worked in UPSCA together, Jimmy as president, and I treasurer. We had many activities, socials and outings in

Jimmy and Mercy in Jerusalem, May 1994

UPSCA. I never had an inkling he would get interested in me, romantically. We were good friends, and I knew him well enough; but it never occurred to me, not once, that there would be any romantic ties.

Recently, when Narita asked me to write about what it is like married to Jimmy, it suddenly occurred to me that it has been twenty-nine years since we exchanged marriage vows at the UP Chapel of the Holy Sacrifice. It may be that our partnership has lasted this long because it was built on our differences.

In so many respects Jimmy and I are dissimilar, and yet, simply by affirming and loving each other, those differences somehow became complementary and so strengthened our relationship.

My husband is a very private person, and I wonder how he would take my candor. I might end up without a husband with this decision to bare his private life. But as a researcher, it is my nature to tell things as they are. Besides, the story of our marriage is also the story of my growing up and maturing. I also want to show the starry-eyed hopefuls that seemingly incompatible people can live a harmonious life together.

FATHER WAS getting tired waiting for me to settle down. In those days, ladies married at around 25 years old, and there I was, already approaching 30. So, when I informed him that I was finally getting hitched to a poet, he was not sure if it was good or bad news. Taking a typically curt but carefully guarded stance so as not to show approval or disapproval, he wryly commented in his trademark Rivera humor, "That is just like taking a vow of poverty. You might as well have entered the nunnery"; for he had discouraged me from entering one.

Actually, he sounded more worried for Jimmy. He asked me if the man had been fairly apprised of my squandering habits; of how badly I handled personal finances. I promised Father I would adjust and adapt, if I had to, to any new standard. I was very much in love, and everything seemed possible. Little did I realize that my father's initial knee-jerk reaction was an understatement.

> *from only Whom shall time no refuge keep?*
> *Though all the wierd worlds must be opened?) Love.*
>   e.e.cummings

Jimmy chose this quote by an eccentric poet for our wedding invitation. I thought then that it was profound. Later, I realized that it was prescient. It did not take a few months to open the "weird worlds" (weird is spelled **wierd** by the eccentric poet) that e.e. cummings hinted at. And I really thought I knew him well enough before we got married: I presumed five years in UPSCA, and another six years after that, including his years as graduate student in the University of Chicago, were enough. But alas! His beautifully crafted love letters and long distance calls on special occasions, or when his meager scholarship allowance would permit, were only the part of his better half. I never really got to know the man until I lived with him, and even after these years, I am still surprised.

It took a few months to demolish my paradigm of an ideal husband which was embodied in my father. I had thought men were like Father, who was a good provider; he was farmer, mechanic, chemist, physician-surgeon, architect, carpenter, mason, sharp-shooter, sportsman, all rolled into one. Father, to me, was the re-incarnation of Robinson Crusoe. I did not think Jimmy would be like him, exactly, but a semblance of my father was good enough for me. Jimmy too, I guess, had his own share of shocks, for I did not know how to cook (not even rice), and he was used to good food, cooked superbly, by no less than his Mom.

It did not take very long for each of us to realize that we were not fairy-tale characters come true. I certainly was not Snow White nor he Prince Charming. These realizations were not carried out in dialogue at that time, but we got a feel of it as the days were lived. I could sense that he expected me to be a housewife par excellance even as I was an Executive at Procter and Gamble. He did not want to be bothered with household details as they interfered with scholarly work. I noticed that he also expected me to take care of all the household details, not the least of which was preparing him a cup of coffee at different times of the day. When I reminded him that I worked, he replied that working was my decision, not his. When I complained about having to make his coffee, and asked if a maid could do it instead, he reminded me curtly that he did not marry the maid. I was very resentful then—I thought his was a rather high and mighty attitude, and the resentment built up in me.

When I got pregnant with our first child, Celeste Aida, the first three months were really bad for me. I vomited most of the time, and I felt nauseated by the smell of garlic, cigarettes and pomade, the last two courtesy of my husband. During this time, I still had to do the cooking, and suffer the aroma of garlic. Jimmy also refused to stop smoking for me. Things were difficult for me then, and I wallowed in self-pity.

I also discovered that the man I married, though erudite and scholarly, was absent when God distributed common sense. He is a total idiot when it comes to using his hands (except for typing and writing, of course). I still clearly remember the first display of his lack of MacGyver skills. The faucet needed changing, and although I knew how to do it myself, I thought it was a job for the man of the house. Jimmy dutifully got a *Reader's Digest* encyclopedia of *How to Fix Things in the House* and followed the instructions faithfully on how to change a faucet. Unfortunately, it did not say anywhere that one should close the main tap first; so, as soon as he removed the faulty faucet, a barrage of water spewed out and spoiled our dining room. I also asked him to put up a frame on the wall. He equipped himself with a hammer but pounded on his thumb instead. He tried again—this time the wall cracked but the nail escaped. Ah, but he did have his brilliant moments...when we had our first flat tire, I watched to see how long it would take him to change the tire—with the help of a manual, it took a little over three hours. Great accomplishment.

Actually, Jimmy has a dread for machines, and I guess the feeling is mutual; machines have a dread for him too, because he mangles them. He dislikes talking through the telephone and specially to an answering machine. He cannot connect anything electronic without help. Cybele, who inherited my nasty tongue, one day told her dad as she was showing him for the nth time how to connect the computer to the printer. "You do not need a doctorate to learn how to do this, dad." Jimmy has given up using his ATM card for he can never remember what his PIN is. There was this funny situation once, when we travelled to the US and left our dollars behind. On the plane, Jimmy assuaged my worry by brandishing his ATM card. When we got to Chicago, we discovered that the ATM card was useless because he forgot the PIN number; in fact, he did not realize that there was one.

Once he drove me to the grocery and noticed that I found the red onions on sale not of good quality; so he pointed to another pile: "Why not those white onions? They look good." He was pointing to a pile of garlic.

What really amazes me is how a simple matter can seem so complicated for Jimmy. He insists I use " precise language". For example, when I talk about Edna, he asks me with a puzzled and half-irritated look: "Edna who?" when, in fact, we only have one close friend named Edna with whom we interact frequently. Things also have to be brought up one thing at a time, or else Jimmy gets upset when I shift too soon from one topic to another without the proper pauses and introductory signals (i.e., when I discuss too many issues one after the other in rapid succession). He finds it disconcerting and rather confusing.

I also realized early in our marriage that while he had released himself from the vows of obedience and chastity, he had not relinquished the vow of poverty which he took as a Jesuit scholastic. Father was prescient, for Jimmy has a simplistic, almost childlike, and totally detached attitude towards monetary and material concerns. Do not get me wrong—he is a good provider for up to now, he gives me everything he earns, and expects me to run his household based on his earnings. The problem is, he is not aware of how much he earns, and has no idea of how much it takes to run a household in this age of two-digit inflation. He does not shop except to buy books and cigarettes. Up to now, he also has to be constantly reminded to get his salary, and each time, he looks surprised that there is such a thing as a salary. Jimmy is probably one of the few men who does not know how much he earns; neither does he know how much he should receive. When President Angara assumed office as UP President, he wanted to know about the UP salary scale, so he asked Jimmy, who then was Secretary of the University. "How much does a person in your position earn?" He surprised President Angara, who was more familiar with Makati sensibilities, by saying he didn't know, he still had to check his contract. Jimmy is oblivious to bonuses or increases due him. When his take-home pay is more than the usual, and I ask him why it is so, he just shrugs his shoulders and says, "Be grateful it is more, not less." I have to ask his secretary or other professors to find out what the bonanza was for.

During the first year of our marriage, I tried my best to live within his income. I did away with my vanities and stopped taking the cab from Quezon city where we lived to Makati where I worked, which had been my habit for many years before I got married. Father warned me to be prudent about my husband's money so that if he should ask for an accounting, it would be nice if he could call me frugal. In the beginning, I wrote down all our expenses, including the money given to beggars. When I review it now, I consider it a feat that we were able to live on 150 pesos a week then. Jimmy is very secure in the belief that God provides even before you ask for it, as He knows exactly what one's need is. Jimmy invokes St. Joseph in a monetary crisis, and I used to mock him and say, "St. Joseph has already sent me to help you." But it fills me with great wonder how this deep faith in God as provider has manifested itself in our lives. Jimmy would rather answer to his Muse's calling and does not work for money. But when we need money badly, it just comes. I have seen it happen many times in our married life.

Jimmy wanted to marry me when he returned from Chicago where he finished his doctorate. The problem was, we had no money. One day, he was invited by a friend to run a two-day seminar, which he did. He did not expect any remuneration for his work, as it was not discussed, but a check for 2,000 pesos resulted from it. I still remember how he fanned the check excitedly in front of me and asked that we move our wedding day six months in advance because he could now afford to marry me. We did get married on 2,000 pesos.

With our second baby, Tosi, we went hospital-hopping, seeking a cure for his disorder. But just the same, he passed away, leaving his grieving parents with debts to six medical specialists. But the money we needed to pay for our baby's hospital bills and specialists dropped straight from St. Joseph through the CCP, which awarded Jimmy's poetry entry 5,000 pesos (second prize). When our third baby, Cybele Lara, arrived prematurely at seven months, we were not ready for the ceasarean operation and the baby's hospitalization. Jimmy took on an extra load, teaching at UP Clark. Much later, we saw this beautiful house in Beverly Hills near Antipolo which we coveted but had no money for. The owner tried his best to make it possible for us to buy his house and was open to term payments. One day, Jimmy came home with some 75,000 pesos which I learned later was a five-year adjustment on his salary as Secretary of the University and the Board of Regents. With that, we made our first payment for the house where we now live.

It has always been this way in our life. Opportunities, positions, and honors come Jimmy's way without his seeking or grasping for them. The funny thing is, he does not always like what others would consider a golden opportunity. For instance, when President Abueva asked him to be Vice-President for Academic Affairs of UP, it took a long resolve on his part before he accepted the position, for he dislikes being an administrator. He would rather be left alone to teach and write poetry, which are what he likes best. When he is sent abroad to travel on official business, he dislikes it too: it brings him away from his family. He gets homesick very quickly.

Jimmy Abad, as director of the U.P. Creative Writing Center

HIS VICES are few—smoking, books, basketball, and the other woman. He stopped smoking in 1984 after a nine-day fast and retreat to protest the repressive and immoral Marcos rule, but he picked it up again later and has been an inveterate smoker since.

Love of books is something we share with a passion, but his is something else. When he is in a book store, the great Abad becomes no different from a boy who has been let loose in Toys R Us. He forgets himself and loses control as his passion takes over. Books have been an irritant in our travels because for him, shuffling through bookstores is the major reason for crossing continents. He also prefers to lug his books in his suitcase and will not mail them because it takes time and lots of prayers before they reach the Philippines safely.

The first time we travelled to Europe, I made the mistake of starting our tour in London, where he feasted on books and spent much of our sparse supply of dollars (foreign exchange was then tightly controlled). He filled his suitcase with books and we had to lug every single one around Europe. One valet commented, "What do you have in here, rocks?" I kept on nagging him to mail his books, so in exasperation he retorted, "What if I mail you instead?" which caused yet another cold war. Once on a British Council grant to Cambridge, having spent all his money on books, he could no longer pay for the excess baggage going home. So, without hesitation, he decided to leave behind his clothing, suits included, rather than part with his precious books. I remember the carpenter who fixed the hinges of his clothes cabinet. He was stricken with wonder when he saw Jimmy's spatter of clothes surrounded by books. He said, "*Ate ngayon lang ako nakakita ng cabinet na mas marami pa ang libro kaysa damit.*" I guess that says it all about his love for books.

In our house, he does not want anyone to touch his books. He arranges, fondles, and dusts them himself, and he knows when somebody messes around with them. The library is a 'sancto sanctorum' which is not to be defiled by illiterates (like the rest of the family, with the exception of Celeste, who is her father's daughter). Jimmy usually wants me working beside him at night, so there is some space set aside for me in his sanctum. As you enter his library, you need not ask where my own space is, for it is one big pile of junk. But mind you, I know where my things are. As I always say, there is order in my disorder. Jimmy, on the other hand, is very orderly, something he says he learned in the seminary. His things are systematically organized and neatly lined up. Since he thinks I am *kalatatoy*, he prefers to keep important family documents, but he keeps them too well; for when these are needed, he has a hard time finding them.

Jimmy cares a lot for books but does not care for clothes. If I do not buy him any, he would not mind nor even notice, and would just continue wearing old ones. He has not heard of color matching either, which his two girls, Cyan and Cybele, often tease him about. Now that the girls are old enough, they help him color-match his wardrobe and socks. Otherwise, it is of no surprise to all in the house if he matches a very new shirt with a tattered favorite pair of pants. When he feels comfortable in his clothes, he wears them over and over until they are worn out.

Come basketball season, I cannot use the television in the house for everyone, from our eldest to our *yaya*, is glued to the game. I cannot talk to Jimmy while his favorite team, San Miguel, is on the court. Whenever I interrupt Jimmy in the middle of a game, I get an irritated look that says it all. He is simply too caught up in the excitement of a game which, I confess, I do not understand. I cannot fathom why the ten big men run up and down the court chasing after an orange ball. I find it rather silly. I always tell him, wouldn't it be simpler if they were each given a ball?

Like any man, there is a second woman in his life. But I must be quick to add that the relationship is platonic. I have long accepted the fact that Ching Dadufalza, his favorite mentor, brings him to intellectual heights I cannot reach. I love to listen to the two of them. I too learn in the exchange.

His driving is out of character, for one who is essentially a mild-mannered and gentle person. Now that I am writing about it, I think it is hilarious. When he is driving, I have to keep reminding him that he is not Steve McQueen. He drives as though the whole world would give way for him, and oftentimes it makes me wonder if he has ever heard of caution. For somebody who does not know the way, he is an aggressive driver. He cannot wait in line (an Abad trait), so he shifts from one lane to the other, toots his horn at the slightest provocation, and gets mad at other mindless drivers whom he assassinates with dagger looks. The two girls feel embarrassed when he toots his horn ("A social embarrassment," they would say) and would attempt at holding him back. Fearing for my safety, very often I feel like step-

The Abad family in Los Angeles, May 1992

ping out of the car, but instead I end up saying harsh words. I can truly say that Jimmy and I hardly quarrel except when he is driving.

The funny thing is that he has a poor sense of direction and does not know his way except to and from his usual destinations, like UP and Ateneo. Send him some place to Makati, he gets lost. We have, on several occasions, found ourselves going the opposite direction of traffic flow on the street. Once a policeman caught him driving the wrong way on a one-way street. When the policeman saw his ID, the officer just broke into an amused grin and laughed out loud. He kept saying "absent-minded professor" or something like that, and sent Jimmy off with a friendly warning not to do it again.

Jimmy's absent-mindedness is getting worse. Lately, he drove around without realizing that he had a flat. If the security guard had not called his attention to the flat tire, he would have driven the car again the next day. When we had the car repaired, the mechanic could not believe that the car still rolled along, and that the driver did not notice at all, what with the rims misshapen to oval. Before this incident, his record incident on being absent-minded was forgetting his passport in New Jersey while boarding in Kennedy Airport, New York. It hardly surprises us anymore when he forgets his car keys inside the car, or if he takes forever to locate his car in a parking lot, or if he forgets to pick up any of the children after class. Actually, back when he was courting me, I knew that he was forgetful—he would forget our date because he got engrossed in a book. But it is always difficult to quarrel with him because he does not fight back.

Jimmy's idea of spending a wonderful day is staying at home in Antipolo—reading, listening to John Denver or Pavarotti, enjoying the breeze and the view of the city, from the window where we see a good vista of Manila and suburbs, or watching the colors of the day change. Our children, too, have picked up this inordinate love for books and are themselves bibliophiles.

People who see us now might think we've had it too easy. On the contrary, the first few years were difficult and I contemplated going home to Father. After I had tearfully told Father why my marriage would not work, and why I was so unhappy, Father commented, "Of course (you are different)—he is an Abad, you are a Rivera." He asked me this one question: "Do you still love him?" I sensed that Father was not too eager to take my side, and was telling me that nothing was wrong with my husband; rather, something was wrong with the way I looked at things. He was not too keen on getting me back home. Taking Father's cue, I slowly let go of the expectations I had accumulated. Having done that, Jimmy was free to be himself and, over time, I understood him and accepted him for himself. Thank God there is no divorce in our country, for if there was, I would have filed one then, and it would have been a most unhappy ending.

Over and above these petty day-to-day considerations, Jimmy's person rises like the proverbial phoenix. Inside, he is a beautiful man predicated on solid values and uncompromising character. Actually, it is during times of crisis that one gets to know a person better, and in our trials and difficulties, I realize I could not have married a better man. Jimmy is kind, loving, and totally there for his family.

His kind of loving is not demonstrative, nor is it the type Hallmark cards enshrine. He loves by respecting my difference and letting me be myself.

I have long stopped dreaming of getting flowers or gifts on anniversaries which he never remembers anyway. Occasionally, I am gifted with a poem which I half understand. Jimmy does not believe in Valentine's day which he says is a product of too much commercialization. According to him, with us, everyday is Valentine's Day. To a certain extent that is true, for he is so available and accessible to me and his children. He is a man of few words and hardly says much, unless you engage him in a discussion. I have lived 29 years with this man, and I still have to see some deviousness or malice in his heart. He seems so pure and simple, I keep on thinking he must be so pleasing to his Creator. All he wants to do in life is to be faithful to his Muse. He exemplifies total fidelity and constancy to his craft and his family. He could easily be a Trappist monk who, in addition to the usual priestly vows, takes a vow of silence and a vow to stay put in one place.

Jimmy lets me be in my career, unhampered. His attitude is that I can do anything I want, provided I do not neglect him, his family and his household. Because he allows me total freedom, the creativity of the universe flows through me. By being himself, I was driven to look at my inner resources and in the process developed some of my talents which I did not even know existed; and I can truly say that I have become a better person.

It has not been easy running a company and a household at the same time, but with the help of others, this has been made possible. A common question that resurfaces over and over is whether any feelings of insecurity have risen, given the fact that I earn much more than he does. Frankly, he does not care. His sense of self-worth is not in any way anchored on titles or earning capacities. Besides, he does not know how to count, figuratively and literally. (You can ask the children to verify that!)

Whatever his limitations are, just as I have mine, I can see that Jimmy has tried very hard in his own way to meet me half-way. He has learned to make his own coffee after some twenty years, so I hope that, God willing, he will learn to make tea in the next twenty-five. When the twins David and Diego came to our lives, it was very difficult for me, even with a nanny to help. Jimmy has tried his best to be helpful, with whatever knowledge and understanding he has on bringing up children. He dotes on the twins and has been more involved in their upbringing than he was with the two girls, whom he found too delicate.

We are two unique individuals, each with different but equally important gifts to offer. Through time, we have learned to affirm our relationship harmoniously. Our deep and enduring love for each other brightens our lives and the lives of our children. Thinking about it as I write this, Jimmy is one of the important resources of my spiritual strength. He is my steady direction and light where I always know myself again. His simplicity and detachment keep us anchored to the ground. His uncompromising faith and complete trust in God blesses us all and brings us closer to the divine.

Jimmy with Nick Joaquin, N.V.M. and Narita Gonzalez (photo by Marra Llanot Lacaba)

Jimmy firmly believes with childlike faith what the mystic Julian of Norwich wrote, "All shall be well, and all manner of thing shall be well." But I think, what has brought us together is simple mathematics: one half-nut plus another half-nut makes a whole nut.

Concepcion Reynoso Angeles
The Writer's Wife

Being married to a writer is no different from being married to any other man who is not a literary man, in the sense that you meet, court each other, marry and raise children, just like anybody else. There may have been differences between the writing life and the ordinary professional or non-professional life, but it made little difference to me. There may have been differences between my husband's life as a writer and his life as a professional, but it made little difference to me.

The family of Carlos Angeles lived on the same street where I lived in San Nicolas, Pasig, Rizal. Our family had been long time residents in that area, while Carlos' family was a relatively newcomer in that town in the early 1930's—the Angeles patriarch being a government official who had been moving from one provincial capital to another because of the nature of his work as provincial auditor.

The Rizal assignment proved to be the longest time spent by the family in any place of assignment in Pasig because, even after the

Carlos and Concepcion Angeles pose for a wedding picture

elder Angeles finished his term of office in Rizal and received his promotion to the Central Auditing office in Manila, the family stayed on in Pasig, which is just twelve miles away.

Carlos' younger sisters were my friends. We all attended the Rizal High School where Carlos was one year ahead in class. He was a staff member of the *Rizalian*, the school paper, where he started writing poetry and did reportorial work for the paper.

In my first year of high school, he started a covert courtship by following me to school, which we usually negotiated by walking the three kilometer distance from our homes in San Nicolas to the school, located in the western part of town the banks of the Marikina River.

Carlos, with American poet laureate of Kentucky Jesse Stuart. This picture was taken at the PEN conference in 1962.

My family had a strict sense of courtship, and my parents may or may not have been aware that Carlos would be cruising the street in front of our house and sneak forbidden glances towards the upper windows where I usually looked out below at the people passing during my leisure hours. In time, he declared his love by writing a love letter, already full of his flowery, poetic and romantic urgings, which I initially spurned because of parental fears. These long-distance courtship with letters (for I did respond only later on) were later on augmented by his following me to school and walking me back home after school hours.

Our love affair was very chaste and he was always a gentleman and a tender suitor who respected me in all ways. It was when were both at the University of the Philippines that we usually met for bus rides home from Manila to Pasig.

When the war broke out in 1941, we had no way of meeting. His family moved to Manila where they had rented a house on Kansas Avenue because his father still worked as City Auditor in the Central Auditing Office. We stayed behind in Pasig.

The war which we thought would last only a year took years to end, and almost all the people were near desperation due to lack of food and other provisions.

I went to hear Mass on June 16, 1944 at the Pasig Catholic Church. He was there, too. I know now, by hindsight, that on impulse, we took this desperation more as the one reason which goaded us to elope and take a chance on marriage although we were both ill-prepared financially to undertake the consequences of married life. We got married at the Manila City Hall, with Judge Almeda Lopez presiding. We then went to his parents' home who were shocked at our daring marital plunge, but took us in without reserve.

But family wanted a church wedding, so we were married all over again at the Pasig Catholic Church on July 1.

The war was now at its decisive stage, and his family transferred to Baguio City, where his father was assigned as City Auditor in the City of Pines for the duration of the war. I was now pregnant with our first child, but the winding year of 1944 saw the Americans victorious in Central Philippines and were pushing on towards Luzon in the great liberation charge that was to oust the Japanese invaders from our besieged land. Liberation from the occupiers now was spreading from Manila northward to the Mountain Provinces where we were, and where the Japanese were making their last-ditch resistance. The American liberators were carpet bombing the mountains of Baguio, and we barely escaped by dodging both liberation bullets and Japanese snipers and escaping through torturous routes over mountains and forests to the lowlands of the Ilocos.

We reached the safety of Tubao in the coastal Ilocos region where we were reunited with Carlos' mother and sister, who were survivors themselves in the battle for the Liberation of Manila earlier that year, and were in Tubao on a chance that we were among the liberated people from Baguio. I was then in my full-term and ready to give birth to our first born. I was thin and under-nourished and I knew my family wondered whether I had survived at all.

I gave birth to our daughter, Cynthia, two weeks after my husband and I reached Pasig. We stayed with my family who, by God's grace, was intact and whole during the liberation period. Carlos' family, who returned to Manila, also was safe and well—so there was general rejoicing in our households.

We had seven children during our long and happy married life. First, of course, was Cynthia, born in 1945; and then Cheryl and Cleanth, who were born one year apart. Charisse was born two years later; then Cedric, born three years later. Carla and Christian were born within three years of each other.

Carlos has always been a good husband and, throughout our married life, a devoted family man to me and our children.

We initially lived with Carlos' parents in the family compound in Paco, Manila, where he first worked as secretary in my brother's printing firm. It was during this time that he started writing poetry in earnest, for money which supplemented his salary as secretary and general factotum in the firm which my family owned.

In 1948, through the initiative of his friend, writer and poet Francisco Arcellana, he joined the International News Service, an American news agency as a reporter. Francisco, whom we fondly call Franz, moved on to professorship at the University of the Philippines, while Carlos stayed on with the foreign news agency. In 1950, when the Korean War broke out, the American boss of the news agency, Frank Emery, was sent to Korea to cover the war. On one of his shuttle plane trips between the warfront and Tokyo, the plane crashed and all aboard were killed. This resulted in a bureau in Manila with no chief to run it. Carlos was tapped by INS to head the bureau, a position he held until the agency, in a merger with United Press, was abolished.

Connie and Carlos in Manila

But before that, Carlos had begun writing poetry in earnest and had developed such writing style that he came to be one of the favorites of editorial offices who published his poems regularly. The money he earn from poetry was actually nothing much, compared to his salary as manager of the news agency.

While head of the INS, Carlos made several connections with the American Embassy people in Manila, some of whom became his sources for news and established close contacts with the Manila publications which were clients of his agency. In 1958 he received a State Department travel grant to the United States where he toured the American east coast and the southern states bordering the Mississipi. He was even made an honorary citizen of New Orleans.

He saw how America could be the land of opportunity for us, and in one of his letters which he wrote while on this tour, he mentioned that perhaps this could be the ultimate goal for him and his family.

Initially, it didn't turn out that way, because soon after he returned from his American tour, the International News Service-United Press merger took place. He and all of his colleagues from INS all over the worldwide system lost their jobs.

He joined the Philippine government by accepting work at the Presidential Press Office. He wrote speeches for President Carlos P.

Garcia during the year he held his position there. Before the year was over, however, he was approached by the American airline, PanAm, to organize and head the public relations office of the company in Manila.

He accepted the position and concentrated on his work with PanAm, where he stayed for 21 years. He totally gave up writing poetry as a result of his commitment to the job he held.

But his passion was poetry. When the children were growing up, he supplemented our income with money from his published works. I remember Carlos would wake up in the middle of the night to work on a literary inspiration until the wee hours of the morning. His works invariably found publication, and what money he got from the magazines he added to the family offers.

The Angeles family

I used to clip every literary work he had and made a scrap book which served as a basis for his first book, *A Stun of Jewels*, in 1964. The book won the first Carlos Palanca award in poetry. He was awarded the Philippine Republic Cultural Award for Literature the same year. Ironically, both awards came during his tenure as public relations official for Pan Am for which he gave up writing poetry.

As a Pan Am employee, Carlos had travel privileges which gave him the opportunity to send the children to the United States where they continued their studies. I travelled a lot to the U.S. and Europe as the spouse of a Pan Am official. (I was able to visit with my children in the U.S. during the years of their residency there, where we maintained a home).

Meanwhile, Carlos' brother, who is a doctor and a citizen of the U.S., had filed a petition for him to immigrate to the United States. There was to be a waiting period of about ten years before Carlos' application for immigrant status in America could be acted on. Since all of our children were already in America, we discussed the possibility of working for the immediate processing of his papers so we could all migrate there. One of my husband's Embassy contacts was a consular officer who suggested that if Carlos filed it from Manila and not through his brother's approved petition, he may be able to make it possible to waive the waiting period to less than a year. While sorely tempted to accept this offer, Carlos still had a few more years to complete in order to merit an early retirement from Pan Am and earn a lifetime privilege of free travel on all lines of Pan Am. So we decided that he defer this generous offer and wait a few more years.

During the height of the Vietnam War, Carlos was sent to Saigon to work there for a few months. But the war got very unbearable and he returned to Manila.

In 1978, when he was officially approved to immigrate to the United States, he filed his papers. But he still had a couple of years to earn to enable him to avail himself of early retirement privileges. He had to shuttle between the U.S. and Manila every six months to maintain his new citizenship status and keep his job at the same time.

Finally, when he reached retirement age in 1980, after 21 years with the airline company in Manila, we pulled up stakes and settled in Los Angeles where most of our children were residing.

His retirement liberated him in more ways than one. He was able to actually savor the benefits of retirement. He may have picked up the urge to write poetry when Doreen Fernandez travelled to Los Angeles from Manila to interview him for a book on writers and their milieu. Then new poems began to be published again. He told me he wanted to put out a collection of his entire poetical works. I know he worked for months compiling the poems which finally saw publication in the collection *A Bruise of Ashes* in 1993.

My husband has always been a writer—from his earliest year as a high school student throughout his collegiate years and adulthood. When it was not poetry, it was the prose of journalism and the public relations fields. He earned from his writings and supported as through the years. We recently celebrated our fiftieth wedding anniversary with seven grandchild attending our anniversary fete.

Oh, yes. My husband the poet had his idiosyncracies when he was creating his masterpieces. He was moody during his creative periods. Despite his moodiness, however, our married life has been a tolerable one.

Connie and Carlos years later

Rose Marie J. Bautista
Joy Bank

We met in Baguio at the St. Louis University. We were both teaching there, Cirilo at the Liberal Arts Department, and I at the Engineering and Architecture Department. This was in 1963-64. He was already a writer then and his poems were being published in magazines. He had a booklet of poems with Albert Casuga, if I am not mistaken. I had read one or two of his poems, and I had heard about him from his teacher in Literature (he was taking his Master's degree then) who thought he was brilliant.

Rose Marie in 1965 before marriage

My feelings about him were that he must be an interesting fellow. Any poet for me, then as now, is always interesting.

I don't believe we had any formal engagement. We started out as friends having a lot of things we enjoyed in common like silence, poetry, painting, and our love of nature. After some months he said he didn't want to go on with the pretense of just being my friend. He said he was in love with me. I was shocked into speechlessness. I had thought then: There goes a beautiful friendship!

After a few months, however, after thinking things over and in spite of everybody's opinion (parents, friends, just everybody including my *labandera* and his had an opinion) that we didn't match, I decided, why not? There are worse things than marrying a friend. He is the one person who, just by his presence, filled up all the emptiness in my heart...I remember telling myself, "Here is a person I can love for always, even if he loses an arm, legs and head." But, then, I had not lived with him yet!

We were married in a very simple ceremony at St. Joseph's Church, Pacdal, Baguio. The only people present were the priest, our two sponsors, Sister Angelina, my former teacher and a friend from St.Theresa's College, and June Ongsangsoy, a mutual friend. We didn't invite anyone because our parents didn't know about it. My parents didn't think it was a smart idea to marry an artist; in other words, they did not approve.

We have three children—Ria, Laura and Nikos. Two of then were born in Baguio; the boy, Nikos, was born when we transferred

The young Bautista couple

to Quezon City. We both wanted to start a family at once because we had no family in Baguio. So were delighted when Ria was born. Coming from a family of seven children, I wanted a big family, too. I dreamt of a dozen children. Cirilo, of course, did not approve. How would we feed, clothe and educate so many children? And when Nikos got asthma, I had to admit it was not a practical idea.

Cirilo is a wonderful father, in the sense that he stopped whatever he was doing whenever the children asked him something. He answered them with patience. During summer vacations, when I had classes and he was free, he stayed with the children in the cottage by the sea, telling them bedtime stories, which were actually the Greek classics. But he had moods. Most of the time, coming from work, he would be so tired that the kids would scamper to their room upstairs. He would not have anything to do with them until after he had a shower. Only then would they show themselves, and we would eat together. During the early years of our marriage, a lot of things must have seemed a burden to him. Cirilo looks at everything, from concerns for now to those of the future. I look at and take things one day at a time, relishing every moment.

Aside from Niko's asthma, the children were no problem. They were quiet and could entertain themselves endlessly. They had creative games; with a fling of an arm, they could be transported to other planets and magic kingdoms. Cirilo was my life but the children were my love and my joy during those early days. I played with them, bathed them, fed them and put them to sleep. Cirilo encouraged this. He, at this point, believed it was a mother's duty to take care of her children. He loved to hear our laughter. When I loved his children, it was proof in his view that I loved him too.

The best way I could handle Cirilo's moods was to ignore them and get on with my life. I had my teaching job which, until these past two years, always had to be part-time because of the children. I had my students, some whom were grown-ups, and were very interesting. I had co-teachers who being designers, were creative in speech and ideas. My life was full with my children and my teaching. Because of these, Cirilo's moods and tantrums could be more easily ignored.

When Cirilo won awards (those were the Palanca awards for poetry and short stories) he was happy and I was happy for him. Anything that makes him an easier person to live with. So I thank God for these awards. That was all they meant to me. I knew what he was worth. I did not need awards to tell me this. but the travels were fun.

The couple in San Francisco, 1980

Those travels were what constituted my Joy Bank, from where I withdraw happy thoughts during my emotional rainy days. Cirilo and I forget all our worries and work when we are away on vacation. We just enjoy each other's company like the old times when we were not yet married. For, during all these years, we have remained friends.

I don't think his writing is an obstacle to our knowing each other. Actually, his writing is a means of knowing him more. But if you mean the time taken up by his writing, the answer is that Cirilo is not the kind of person who shuts himself up in the room to write. He shuts himself up in the room because he has this big thing about privacy. He also closes all windows and doors. What I do is simply open the windows and doors.

What I am trying to say is that Cirilo is a very private person. He has a lot of secrets; he thinks, or he likes to think. Knowing that there are things that people don't know about him makes him happy.

I don't consider his writing a competitor. I am too busy doing my own thing to resent the time he spends in writing. But our social life is close to nothing. He does not accept invitations which my friends give. Oftentimes, I have to go alone or with other friends. But I am used to this now. Actually, going out partying is not my idea of a good time either. What I enjoy is going out with Cirilo, even if this is just to buy books or watch a movie. What I really look forward to is our one week celebration of our wedding anniversary. We get out of town with the children. Most of the time, this coincides with his summer literary seminars, which is really fine with me because I do enjoy these happenings. What is important is that we are together almost every moment of the day and we have time to renew our relationship.

I think I know him quite well. Knowing does not necessarily mean that I like all I know but that I do understand why he is what he is, and try to accept the things about him which seem unchangeable. He gives me the same privilege and I am grateful for it.

Linda Ty Casper
Being Married to a Writer

There is a quote which maps out a writer's life and work. If I had come upon it earlier, I might have been better prepared for the life Len and I were to have. (I can't decipher the source in my hurried handwriting.) A writer requires "Quite simple things...the time and solitude necessary to temper talent and vision. A little money for supplies. The emotional support of kindly and patient friends. The right historical moment to present his work... a sympathetic critical champion, gently guiding an audience to proper appreciation of the artist's gift... How hard they are to come by, what luck is required in the quest and how rarely artists themselves confront their difficulties in an engaging spirit..."

Len is the first creative writer in my family. (There is my mother who wrote social studies textbooks for the Bureau of Public School, but we did not discover her sonnets until after she died in 1982. And I did not know that Tio Pepe, son of Don Epifanio de los Santos, was a writer until he came to ask us

Linda, Len and their younger daughter

to store his father's papers and his.) When Len first came to the house in Malabon in the early fifties, he brought me a book of poetry as *pasalubong*. I ascribed the unusual gift to his being a writer. These were the first poems I did not have to read and be tested on in class. He was also shy. This, too, I assumed was because he was a writer.

Len came to the Philippines mainly on the promptings of several Filipino writers he met at Stanford where he ws a creative writing fellow. One of these was Amador Daguio. So, after returning to Cornell where he was teaching while finishing his doctorate at the University of Wisconsin at Madison, and instead of going on to London on a Fulbright research grant, Len boarded a freighter for the Philippines.

In Cornell, a haberdasher had advised Len to bring a tuxedo— for partying at Manila Hotel and for walking on the seawalls of Luneta, a drink in hand; cotton cord suits for ordinary occasions. Once he got to Manila, Len realized how out of place those clothes were for a writer and teacher. He began wearing plain shirts.

Len received an appointment to teach at the University of the Philippines on the strength of his doctorate and his publications, which were both creative and academic. Besides poems, he had published short stories. One was included in the O. Henry anthology, and in *The Best American Short Stories of 1951*. (His short stories received a National Council on the Arts award in 1971 and were published under the title *A Lion Unannounced*, by Southern Methodist University Press the same year.)

Len was soon writing reviews of Philippine literature for *Panorama*, Dean Vicente Sinco's publication which Fel Santa Maria edited. Early on Len realized the importance of teaching Philippine literature side by side with American and English literature at the University. At NVM Gonzalez' instigation, he edited a book of poems, *Six Filipino Poets*. Also during his first stint at the U.P., Len brought out *Wayward Horizon* which, with some prefaces he had written for Philippine collections, he expanded into *The Wounded Diamond*, 1964.

The Caspers with Tina and sister Gretchen and her husband

From 1953 to 1956, Len taught at U.P.. When he came to visit he would mention the writers he had met and what he was working on. I never before realized how labor-intensive writing is; still, instead of spending one's time in endless small talk and frivolous entertainment, one had a poem or a short story, something that did not exist before you wrote it. It was, I felt, like discovering fire all over again, each time. Before I met Len, I had the impression that writing was self-indulgent, an excuse to avoid serious work. The fact that one writes, not primarily to make money or for rewards—it's not cost-efficient as production lingo goes—made it even more appealing, so I thought of becoming a writer myself. But I had exams and papers and no time really. Anyway, I did not think I could ever succeed because writing seemed almost to be "taking part in a mystery," so single-minded and intense was the effort, almost heroic.

Our engagement was short, compared to Philippine expectations at that time; but we first met in 1953 so when we thought of getting married in 1956, the time period was reasonably respectable. I had no way of knowing what to expect, marrying a writer. I knew it would probably mean letting my own career go. The hardest part was that we were going to the United States soon after the wedding. I had never been away from home, not even to live in the dorm the six years I was at U.P..

The wedding was simple. Fr. Pacifico Ortiz arranged to celebrate it at the Archibishop's Palace, which was small. There were mainly relatives because Len insisted on paying for the wedding with his U.P. salary. There were so many things to worry about besides the wedding. We were not certain when my father would return from helping arrange for the reparations to the Philippine national railways, yet we had to be in the United States in time for the first semester in the Fall, because I was going to Harvard and Len had received an appointment to Boston College on the strength of the letter of Father Kunkel to the Executive Vice-President of B.C.. To the Dean of Arts and Sciences, Father Charles Donovan, Father Miguel Bernad sent a personal letter.

Linda's latest photo

J.D. Constantino, then teaching at MIT, picked out an apartment for us in Cambridge but we arrived a day late and ended up in a so-called three-room apartment which was really a single storefront divided into three. The dining table was underneath the stairs to the second-floor apartment. Our front door could not be opened if the upper-floor tenants left their door open against ours. But we were in time for classes and I had my green card and transcripts in order. There was no time to look back.

We walked a lot from Harvard Square to our North Cambridge apartment. Len got a ride to B.C. with John McAleer who lived on the next block. Thus we saved on subway fare. We could not afford a car on Len's salary as assistant professor (a minimal $4400) and he would not accept any help from my parents. Sometimes, the chairman, Ed Hirsh, would take us back across the Charles so we could attend special activities on campus. T.S. Elliot gave a lecture almost every year. Robert Frost read his poems. We did not feel disadvantaged since everyone we knew was living unpretentiously, though some faculty had large houses in Newton and nearby suburbs.

Len liked the collegiality at Boston College, so without making a definite decision, we found ourselves staying; moving to Watertown (once the capital, during the Revolution) then to a Cape house of our own in Saxonville. Modest moves. We could not afford to live near the college. Someone told us that Saxonville, miles west, was safe, in case the Russians dropped a bomb on MIT, and missed. Besides, the house we bought was on the Sudbury River.

Gretchen was two when we moved to Saxonville so she could have space to play in. She was born in Watertown. Indicative of my family's concern was their offer of a helper. Even then, I realized it would not be in keeping with our way of life, and refused. U.P. classmates could not believe I washed the dishes. One received a scholarship to study in the States but refused since she would have to take care of her laundry.

We were determined to be independent, but people were kind to us. Our Canadian landlady (who would go to Cananda and donate a $6000 organ to her church, without batting an eyelash) offered to babysit for Gretchen, any time, for free. Close to ninety then, she would knock at our door around five in the morning with a plate of freshly-made doughnuts. When, after two years, we decided to buy a house, Lotte tried to persuade us to stay. We were able to summer in Rhode Island because a friend would have us to stay at her house, at minimal cost, just so we would not feel like charity cases, and we had the run of her house and her garden. Often we returned from a day trip to Connecticut to find she had dinner waiting. When I had to return to the hospital, Len would take Gretchen in her bassinet to Margaret and Ed Hirsh, on his way to classes at B.C.. When Chit Dadufalza was at Radcliffe, she would come over to make *adobo*. And, of course, packages came regularly from friends and relatives in the Philippines, with clothes for Gretchen and me, with cans of *macapuno*, specially-canned *bangus* and *bopis*, delicacies I could never cook in the States.

Our first home-cooked meal in Cambridge was a lunch of sardines. We had breakfast at a small restaurant on Massachusetts Avenue and were embarrassed to return for lunch and admit we were inept at the stove. It took me a long time to really cook so it was canned meats for a while. Until we discovered meat pies, it was spaghetti, corned beef hash and the CARE rations from home. Eating out, we discovered quickly, ruined our budget.

Anyway, I found out that writers pay no attention to things they can do without. They want only to write well, and the simpler the life, the better for writing. We made do, and it was fun most of the time. An aunt visited us in Saxonville, was aghast that we had only one house to show for the years we were in the States. A niece of hers in California had bought several houses for rental purposes after being in the States half the years we had been there. For us, business and writing did not mix. I remember my father telling my sister, "If you enter the government service, do not go into business as a sideline. Your loyalty becomes divided between your work and your profit." When our friend in Rhode Island, Gladys Lillibridge, inherited land from her father, she offered to sell us an acre or more, fronting Larkin Pond, at half-price. But we would not, financially or emotionally, afford a second home.

Moving to Saxonville was the best thing we managed to do. We still live there, along the Sudbury River, which joins the Charles somewhere in Concord where there is a bird sanctuary. We see herons and waterfowl, on their way to nest or to summer South. And while we can see the neighbors when we step out the front door, from the back there is only the river and the trees, as if we were out in the country. In any other place, writing would have been impossible; we'd be looking into the neighbor's backyard. Len kept adding hedges and trees so that Gretchen complained, "In this family, every time there is money, it goes into a shrub." But for years the girls enjoyed ice skating in the winter on the Sudbury, which in the fall and spring is full of migrating birds.

Both Kristina and Gretchen wanted to write when they were growing up. Now that they are both married and living away from home, when I attempt to clear their rooms, I come across their poems or stories, some with illustrations, marking the years of their growing up. Gretchen's short stories placed in national contests. One was a finalist in a *Scholastic Magazine* competition; another was an honorable mention in *The Writer's Digest* contest. Now they are both into academic work. Gretchen's first book is coming out in early 1995. Entitled *Fragile Democracies: Legacies of Authoritarian Rule*, it is based on months of interviews with church and military officials in the Philippines where she returned, on her own, several times. Pittsburgh University Press has the option on her second book which is almost complete, so she is planning a third. Kristina, who, while in high school, was writing a science fiction novel, is now writing her thesis on "handedness" in primates. She complains that in her scientific writing class she finds herself writing creatively.

The children's interest in writing did not prevent them from sometimes resenting the fact that because Len always had writing to do—articles, books, an anthology of world literature which went into several editions, reviews for the *Boston Herald* and for journals, entries for encyclopedias and, occasionally, a short story—there were activities their friends were doing as a family, like camping, that we did not have time for. But we did enjoy trips to the Philippines as a family. Though Len would be on a Fulbright grant, we always exhausted our savings because of the plane fares and the trips to Europe on the way back. (Pan Am gave travelers then the option of going around the world—stopping at eleven cities—instead of returning the same way over the Pacific.) This way the girls saw Hong Kong, Singapore, Bangkok, Istanbul, Teheran, along with the usual cities in Europe.

Whatever recognition Len has had are hard won, teaching had replaced writing poetry and short stories for he had to write academic books for promotion, but his way of writing also needed solitude since he was writing within himself, reinventing language to link experiences of life with those in texts. The work forms in the mind which can be distracted and absorbed by other things. Many times, he would not want to have friends over for dinner because he had something in his mind. I also discovered that friends had invited us, through him, but he did not let me know. Whatever invitations came from or via Boston College fell by the wayside.

But the times we went, Len enjoyed himself. His shyness melted. Once, Helen Cort, whose husband John was Peace Corps director when we were in the Philippines at one time, called. I gave the usual excuse (we had another engagement, not that Len was writing because that did not seem like a normal reason not to go). "We're also

N.V.M. and Narita and the Caspers, at their home in Saxonville, Massachusetts

inviting you. Come by yourself if Len can't make it." It never occurred to me to do that.

However, life is not only to write. A writer has to remain connected to the world which is the nourishing source, but too much and it takes over, absorbs the writer. The question of striking the right balance is never achieved once and for all times. Distance and detachment, though ideal for writers, are not always possible. This is not the same as indifference which is stifling.

So hours and days and weeks have often gone by without any writing. Being with friends, going to museums, to historical places, to playgrounds and parks—all day trips, usually—did not stand in the way of writing when it started to come. When it did, Len needed to be by himself—he would be cranky anyway—so his work could express his individual and unique way of seeing and writing and could not be harmed by constant shift of focus and a flood of outside interactions and information.

If he is not writing, Len was reading widely about the Philippines. We gradually accumulated over a thousand such books. Len's interest in Philippine literature in particular, resulted in his putting together books of essays on the subject, in his writing introductions to several collections, or even just going over manuscripts to make recommendations about which prices to include and in what sequence. His hope that objective and impersonal criticism would help advance the cause of Philippine literature is affirmed by the publication of several new books of criticism appearing in the Philippines by younger writers.

Looking back, there is little I would want to have differently. Though living in the States, we have met people we would have been poorer in spirit if missed. Our first family doctor, from two towns away, was a real friend. Once I rushed Gretchen there by taxi, thinking she had smallpox, and he brought me home to save me the fare, and because I was upset enough to mistake some mosquito bites for the pox. Our neighbors look after the house when we go on trips. (We rented the house out only once and was burned by the experience. The man stripped the paintings from their frames in order to burn these for firewood, along with some pieces of furniture, and left cigarette marks on the rest. A neighbor alerted us that something was not quite right.)

Our visits to the Philippines (while Len was on sabbatical) were always special. These enabled my family to keep up with the children's growth. There are delightful memories. Once, a ninety-year old aunt called to me, "Tina is talking to me but I can't understand her Tagalog." Kristina was speaking in English with her Tagalog accent.

Each time, we met other writers, renewed friendships. I recall one dinner when I felt sick to my stomach before it was served. Estrella Alfon calmly cut a small thin slice of butter to hand to me. "This has always worked," she assured me. In the course of those visits, Len was able to teach not only at U.P. and Ateneo, but also at the Philippine Normal College (besides giving lectures in others), my mother's alma mater. He became acquainted with many of her classmates. In workshops, Len met the young writers. The part of the visit, Len enjoyed very much. I remember, was one instance when I had a stomachache before dinner was served.

Meeting other writers in the States augmented those visits home. Through the years we met the Manuel Virays, the Ben Santoses. Just this year, Father Miguel Bernad came to Boston on his way to research archives in Washington, D.C. and Ann Arbor. While we were sitting in the garden I remembered to ask him to bless the statues of the Virgin that a neighbor had just brought us from Tennessee. I often remember Father Bernad when I see the statue. Then once, close to their fiftieth wedding anniversary, NVM and Narita came to Harvard. We had a short but very pleasant visit into which we were able to fit Lexington via the Great Battle Road from Cambridge, Concord and the Revolutionary landmarks, Longfellow Inn in Sudbury. Roger Bresnahan stayed a couple of days while I was visiting my parents. He took over Tina's room and was kept awake by the posters falling off the walls.

One of the good things about being a writer is having a shelf of one's own books in the house. We keep them in the den/library, not in the living room, so as not to impose on friends.

After thirty-eight years, Len and I are still trying to simplify our lives to give writing more space. I think writing, somehow, reduces natural selfishness. That we can do without many things—do not have to own what we enjoy—is quite liberating. It allows us to share more, to be concerned not only with ourselves. It has become a habit which, though they once chafed it, the girls have also acquired.

We continue to talk about writing, among other things. Often I run across an essay or newspaper clippings pertinent to what Len is writing. Because of what has become our common interest—not that our opinions always coincide—we support each other instinctively. We have never been competitive as individuals—perhaps it is a weakness, but on my side, it comes from my grandmother constantly telling us not to overreach; if God meant you to have or be something, it will happen regardless—so we aren't and have never resented each other's success.

Now that Len has retired (how quickly junior faculty becomes professor emeritus!) and only teaches part-time, we have been able to take trips more readily. So dedicated was Len to his teaching that he would not cut classes except for emergencies. (He was *The Heights* man-of-the-year when he was still an assistant professor at Boston College.) We went to Bangkok for the SEA WRITE Award ceremony in 1993. Earlier that year, we went to the Holy Land and Spain. The following year we were both at the Bellagio Writing Center under the auspices of the Rockefeller Foundation. A recurring problem with ruptured disc has kept us in Saxonville. It is difficult for others to understand why enforced rest does not "drive us crazy." Recuperations after operations, and retirement allow us to focus on writing, on reading.

I'm hoping Len returns to creative writing now. We are discovering, however, that time and energy slip away unnoticed when there are no deadlines and set schedules to meet.

I have to remind Len that he can't keep reading manuscripts of friends' friends or those that people, met casually, thrust upon him when they learn that he teaches writing and he's a writer. He has received no acknowledgment for material he has analyzed; the critique was really not welcome, since only praise was expected. One Northeastern professor, a good friend of a friend, requested that Len look over his manuscript that had been rejected by publishers. Len practically had to rewrite it. When his university finally published it, no credit was given for Len's work, no copy of the book either. But then, after Len worked on his manuscript, he did not bother to call. He even asked Len to bring it to his house because his wife had the car.

Those, I tell Len, do not deserve his time and energy because they are not real writers. Real writers are not self-centered. They make available to all the significance they achieve. Not after sensation through falsified feelings, they try to preserve what might otherwise be lost of people's lives, and the life of their country. They are too deeply committed to literature and everything implicated in it, that they do not pass on ideologies but give readers something to think about, helping them to arrive at the truth about themselves. Our writings are where we live on, until mortal time ends because at its heart is refinement beyond manners, and integrity.

Rosalina Icban Castro

To My Darling Wife

※⟨G⟩※

I learned almost halfway through my 46 years of marriage to the writer-newspaperman Jose Luna Castro that if I gave him the upper hand in our marriage, he'll let me be the "queen" of our home. One of the few cards he gave me just before he died in 1986 sums up his feelings for his wife: "...to my darling wife, am I a lucky son-of-a-gun."

Joe and I had very similar family backgrounds. We were both Preachers' Kids (PK), our fathers being two of Pampanga's first Methodist preachers at the turn of the century.

Being both poor, we could not go to the big school in Manila when we were ready for college. We were sent instead to the Union College of Manila, the college department of the Union Theological Seminary on Taft Avenue. There we were together for four years. Our advantage was our teachers were mostly American missionaries—and many of them were really outstanding. Take our English teacher, Alice Mary Johnson, a Phi Beta Kappa from Oberlin College. She mothered us. She even offered to pay for Joe's college diploma. Another was Dr. Hibbord, who became Silliman

The young Castro couple

University's President Emeritus.

Joe's mother, a very pious Methodist lay wanted her son to follow in the footsteps of his minister-father. "He must train at the Union Theological Seminary after his college education," she said.

However, Joe was able to convince his mother, with the help of some American missionaries, to allow him to go into the writing profession instead. He had written short stories for *Graphic Magazine* which won for him inclusion in Jose Garcia Villa's Honor Roll in the early 40's. And for extra money, he wrote articles, sometimes using various pen-names. He was very prolific.

The Castros and three children. Their oldest is not in the picture

And so, one day his mother gave him some money to get himself a typewriter. He went to a British shop which sold typewriters but he did not have enough money to pay for it and he walked away disappointed.

The British salesman stopped him and asked. " Aren't you getting your typewriter?"

"I don't have enough money," he answered.

"Then I'll give you a rebate," the salesman said.

"What's a rebate?"

"A discount."

So with the "rebate" from the kindly-looking salesman, he went home the happiest of men.

We got married in 1940, on his birthday, March 4th. He was exactly 25 years old, and I was two and a half years younger. The church was bare save for two tall vases of pink gladiolas on the sanctuary. I wore a white dress that I designed myself. It was inspired by the many Franciscan monks who strolled in groups of two or threes every afternoon on the wide Luneta. My dress had a cowl similar to theirs.

We had no wedding march, no flower girls, no best man. It was a very little affair strictly for two immediate families. Just about a dozen people were there. But I remember the beautiful organ music in the background.

We had no reception. From the church, I had to rush to the Little Theater of U.P. in Manila to participate in a play written and directed by Professor Augusto Catanjal. (I was in Graduate school there.)

Joe must have been very mad at such an arrangement but I think NVM Gonzalez, who was the only outsider at the wedding and who kept Joe company at the Little Theater, quieted him down.

And that is how we started our life together. With the little money we had, we bought furniture for our little place at 594 San Luis Street, a one-bedroom affair, part of the parsonage where we stayed at no expense because our American pastor and his wife went home on furlough.

Although I had ambitions of becoming a writer myself as a young girl in Tarlac, I was completely overwhelmed by this guy who wrote prize-winning stories. So frightened was I by the thought of ever attempting to write that for the next thirty of forty years I did not pursue the little dream I had of seeing my name in print.

It wasn't easy getting adjusted to this man, who was very strong-willed and extremely bossy. When I complained about certain things he did, he'd say, "Remember, I am older than you, and I know better."

With all the quarrels that came, I found it very difficult to cope. I was brought up by most loving, gentle parents, unused to all the harsh situations that came regularly in my new home.

One day I decided to go back home. I packed my clothes in my *baul*, a wooden trunk. "What's all this?" he asked.

"I am going back home."

"Hurry," he said, "so I can pack you in too."

Half of the years we were married we quarreled about little things, mostly. He did not like the way our driver drove the car. He did not like the way the maid scrubbed the floor. In the mornings he expected me to be close by so I could make his coffee.

One time he found me in the garden very early that morning when I should have been inside the house waiting on him. He took the water hose and gave me a water hose bath!

What was I to do with this marriage? Deep in my heart I really loved the man. And so I said to myself I must do something!

So I decided to change course. I must play dumb. I must never answer back.

To my great surprise, the quarrels diminished slowly. No more shouting in the middle of the night. If he burnt the night table with his cigarette butts, I did not say a word. I stopped nagging him about his smoking. I stopped asking why he came home late, after working hours, in the wee hours of the morning.

Of course, I decided to change because I loved the man and I knew he loved his family too—his two children, Ianthe and Dave.

With the change in me, I found out he quieted down slowly. I gave him all the attention, showed him I did care for him. I stopped complaining about anything.

Did he want me to stop teaching? If he said yes, I would have done so immediately.

And as the years passed by, he became so tame, so loving. He wanted his wife with him wherever he went.

Once he was invited to go to Japan and he wanted me along.

"Please," I said, "I have diarrhea."

"You must come. All will be well."

And so I went. To my amazement, the diarrhea stopped. Pictures of our group showed, to my embarrassment, that I was the only woman in this group of Filipino and Japanese newsmen.

And from then on, it was smooth sailing. He invited friends to

The Castros with all the children: Ianthe now teaches at U.P.

the house and took me to their homes. He took the whole family to basketball games, to picnics. He took me to dinners for two, and overnight stays in big hotels.

I was with him on his visit to England for a whole month, seeing plays in London and Stratford-on-Avon. We went to France and Germany. We went to Taiwan and made a lot of friends. Then to Beijing for two years in the 70's, to San Francisco, to D.C.. We had the happiest of times.

One thing I'd like to say, I never—in all our years together—did attempt to compete with my husband to show that I could be on my own, that I could be better, maybe. I completely subordinated myself to him.

And during all this time after he had gone, I've done a little writing myself, talking about our happy life together, the places we visited, the joys of family, children (we had four in all) and grandchildren as well. And I fulfilled my little dream, too.

I am glad I found courage and faith and common sense before it was too late to change the course of our life together, which thank God, turned out to be a very happy one for all of us in the family and our many friends as well.

Remedios Calma Cruz
The Wind Beneath His Wings

※※☙☕❧※※

I have been married to a writer for almost twenty-seven years. Our life together has been eventful and exciting, with considerable mobility, diverse experiences, and changes in lifestyle. I have not regretted it, but there were times in the past when I wondered if a more sedate life would have been better. To be honest, I sometimes questioned the soundness of my decision to marry someone in this profession. The "flaw" in the decision could be due to our youth (I was twenty-two; he was barely twenty-five when we got married), or to the short courtship (We dated for less than three months). Or, I could say that the difficulties we had in the early years were not entirely due to his love for writing. All three are very likely true.

There are many myths or misconceptions, if you will, about writers. The stereotype would be a bohemian, with a cigarette in one hand and a drink in the other. It is said that writers, who also fancy themselves as intellectuals, like to congregate and drink

Isagani, Medy and first born

well into the night, discussing matters of great import. Shades of Paris and New York. "Starving artist" is also a common appellation, although it would probably apply more to people whose only source of livelihood is their craft. Throughout our marriage, many people we have met would fit this stereotype in some way. My husband does not, which may explain why our marriage has lasted. He does not smoke; he does not drink. He falls asleep after one bottle of beer or a glass of wine. And from the very beginning of our marriage, he has regarded writing as an interest, an avocation; never his main source of income.

MARRIAGE IS hard work, but marriage to a writer is harder. No, there is nothing particularly wrong about being a writer. But writing attracts a certain kind of person, a particular specie of homo sapiens; it is life with this person that is difficult. Anyone who marries this individual must be willing to adjust, to make concessions, to love the lifestyle that marriage to this person will bring.

Perhaps it is wrong to generalize. There are, after all, many

The Cruz family

different kinds of writers; each one will be different from the next. After meeting a number of writers, however, I am reasonably certain that writers share common traits, certain characteristics that are more apparent in them than in others with a different occupation. Although I will claim that my husband is unique, I will concede that he has many things in common with other writers.

Our older daughter thinks that our marriage is one of the best she has seen (not that she has seen that many), and I tend to agree. Today the marriage is stable, the two of us comfortable with who and what we are in relation to each other. He likes to think of himself as a "kept man", and although there is some truth to it because I take care of all household expenses, he more than earns his keep. The fact that he can laugh about it and talk about it tells me that he does not suffer from any dents to his male ego because I earn more than he usually does. Our marriage today is given to a lot of laughter, sharing, hugging, and arguing.

I once remarked to my husband that writers are quite arrogant and bigoted. He admitted as much, saying that writers must believe that they are right and that their views are better than everybody else's. It is this strength of conviction that spurs them to write. I agree whole-heartedly, considering the nature and number of arguments that we have had. If there is one word I will use to describe my husband, it is "opinionated." His smugness, his arrogance urges me to discuss (argue) with him on every conceivable topic—from a debate on practitioners versus academics or theorists, to the use of language in education, or to the amount of cool air a car-airconditioner can generate. The blame is not entirely his, however; I have a contrary streak two miles wide.

Being an equally opinionated person who likes to win arguments, I find it humbling that I have never won a square argument with my husband. I have proven him wrong on many occasions, but I have never won an argument based on pure logic. Since I am a poor loser, I sometimes resort to throwing fits and tantrums just to win the argument. It is a good thing that I am a woman because had I been a man, he would have hit me on the occasions when I was extremely ornery. He has told me, however, that the reason he has never hit me is because he knows I will hit him back, and my right hook would probably be stronger than his.

I have often said that women are not illogical; their logic is merely different. Well, my feminine logic is no match against my husband's logical steel-trap of a mind. As in chess, he waits for flaws in my arguments then pounces on these. Not even my knowledge of business and management can stand up to his theoretical constructs. Experience and reality can be easily demolished by theory and logic. It is unfortunate that he cannot accept that most people do not act in accordance with the dictates of logic. He is, after all, an idealist, a theorist who provides the world with a mirror of its own absurdity in his writings. It is not a coincidence that my husband's interest in the theater focused for a number of years on the works of Ionesco and Albee.

Contrary to common belief, not all writers are emotional and operate only at the intuitive level. My husband is one exception. His marriage proposal to me, for instance, was in the form of a logical proposition. If statement A (he loves me) is true, then B (he cannot stay in the priesthood) must be true, etc. This logical view of the world is reflected in the orderliness and structure that he applies to everyday life. His schedule, his things, his possessions, his books— all these are arranged with infinite care and monitored or cleaned religiously. He records everything. He has a notepad in his pocket, in his briefcase, on his desks (at the office and at home), in his car, and in the bathroom. I do know that this is not unusual. Many writers jot down their observations and their thoughts in a notebook that they have with them at all times. It is doubtful, however, that other writers are as meticulous and orderly as he is, or as obsessed about documenting everything. His side of the room and the house, although filled with books and papers, is always neat. There are piles of stuff, but these are neatly stacked and properly labeled.

This obsession with order and planning is at odds with a strong romantic streak which I love dearly. He is also thoughtful; he sends me cards on every conceivable occasion. (It is I who sometimes forget certain events, such as his birthday). He sends me flowers all the time, then complains later about the bills from the florist since he is at the same time a frugal person. There was one Valentine's Day when he was tempted to buy flowers that his students were selling (he is a professor, too) at rock-bottom prices. When I saw them that evening, the flowers were worse than dead. He felt so embarrassed that the following day I received more than a dozen long-stemmed roses. He claimed these were the ones he really wanted to give me. There was another time when we went to a function driving our separate cars because we came from two different locations. I was behind him, and had just stopped at a traffic light when a boy selling flowers suddenly appeared at my window. He handed me a rose, saying that the man in the car ahead had bought it for me. He looked confused, probably not understanding why a middle-aged man would give a rose to an unknown middle-aged woman. I laughed all the way to the house.

I suppose this romantic nature, this capability to be unconventional, or to disregard society's approval, is one characteristic that he shares with other writers and artists. Although he is highly predictable, this romantic side, as well as his sometimes extreme views, makes life with him more interesting, and sweet.

A WRITER'S household is organized differently. The schedules follow a different clock and are organized around a different set of rules.

My husband writes early in the morning. He wakes up before dawn, then writes until past six o'clock. This schedule requires him to sleep early, usually before nine o'clock. I, on the other hand, like to go to bed late although I wake up at about six o'clock. In the early years this habit bothered me because he works in our bedroom. I would wake up when the lights were turned on, and would find it difficult to get back to sleep. I learned to adjust to this, first by putting the pillow over my head, or by putting on a blindfold, a sleep mask. When he bought a computer to replace his typewriter, I was quite happy, until the printing sounds woke me up. He has since learned to postpone printing until the time I wake up.

Because he prefers to write early in the morning, we had to move from the suburbs into the city. Years ago we lived in Parañaque and had to leave the house before seven, which meant getting up by five o'clock. It left my husband very little time to write. Because he could not write as much as he wanted to, he was miserable. He resented staying out there, he resented the traffic we had to go through, and he resented having to take me to work. He resented not being able to attend functions which writers seem to give at the slightest excuse because we lived so far from the city. Since traffic was worse in the evenings, by the time we got home, he would be too tired to write. We quarreled practically everyday.

Medy and Gani abroad

We lasted three years in that brand new house. We moved into an apartment in the heart of the city, breathing polluted air and seeing our furniture turn black from the soot and dust. But my husband was ecstatic. He was one block away from school so he did not need a car. He could leave any time he wanted to, and on days when he had no class, he could write to his heart's content. So, our relationship improved because he was spared the aggravation and the frustration that he used to go through every day.

Writers, I have concluded, can be addicted to their writing. Taking that away from them is like taking away their happiness, their fulfillment. That was a lesson I learned the hard way. To make my husband happy, I had to give him time and the peace of mind to write. All other elements of the marriage became secondary.

We have lived in the city for the last ten years. Today, we are planning our retirement house, but this cannot be too far away from Metro Manila because my husband does not intend to stop writing. He will retire from teaching, but never from writing.

There are many rules that we observe closely around the house. The children cannot play their radios or the television loudly; my husband does not answer the phone in the mornings unless it is from people he needs to talk to; and our bedroom is his sanctuary. His work area is in our bedroom, and the children cannot stay there if he is working. Years ago, I had to protect him from any disruption from the children or the rest of the household. I became adept at taking care of the children's needs, including fixing broken toys. I took care of any minor repairs around the house; I could wield a hammer, a screw driver, and a wrench. I learned how to buy construction materials from the hardware. Today, I have a number of handymen on call for the repairs. But, it is still my responsibility to maintain the house and the cars. I take the cars to the garage for servicing. I have become accustomed to waiting with men—drivers, male relatives, car owners—in the customer lounge of service centers.

I have also learned not to ask his help around the house—lifting things, opening jars and bottles, bringing in grocery bags, etc. The things I can lift or carry, I do myself. When we lived in Maryland where he studied for his doctoral degree, one apartment we stayed in was at the end of the building farthest from the parking lot. It was on the fourth floor, and there was no elevator. On days when I stopped by the grocery store, I would park the car, take out my key, and trudge up the apartment with two or three bags at a time. I had to maneuver the bags to be able to open the apartment door. I never rang the bell even if I knew he was home because he could be writing. Once in, I would deposit the bags in the kitchen, and go back for the rest. I also never asked him to help me take the laundry to the basement.

Today, the only task that he does around the house is replacing light bulbs. This way, he will not feel totally useless. He also takes care of his own work area. He cleans his computer, his desk, and his book shelves. He does not want the maids re-arranging his things, or messing up the wirings in his computer.

Although he writes in the house and therefore works seven days a week, he has designated Sunday afternoons as our family day. To his credit, he has tried his best to keep to this schedule. Whatever writing he does on Sundays, he does this in the morning.

When the children were small they could not understand why an outing would be delayed or cancelled altogether because their father was working. He was in the house; therefore, he was not at work. In fact, there were many holidays when the two girls and I would go on quick trips with my brothers and sisters without my husband. Perhaps age has something to do with it, but in the last few years, he has been more and more insistent that we go out together, as a family. The girls are grown up, and despite his inaccessibility when they were growing up, they are now quite close to him. It helped that he was always in the house. Whenever he surfaced from his writing, he would talk to the girls or play with them.

My efforts to protect his writing from disruption extend to the neighbors. We live in a townhouse building where choosing your neighbors is impossible. I sometimes knock on our neighbors' doors, asking them to turn down their stereos or radios even during the day. Although they know as well as I do that I have no right to do this, they have been most cooperative.

His nightmares are mine, too. During that terrible year of fre-

when the power was cut un-
vhen his computer gave way
nce gave him my entire mid-
iter. If the roof leaks, I worry
r. If the leaks are elsewhere,
he repair. Since he is impos-
I make sure that everything

ed to see my name in what-
l has dedicated his works to
it I have had the privilege of
My name appears sometimes
ince many columnists write
al lives as illustrative mate-
I am mentioned in the "Ac-
edit his works. I enjoy doing

w stable of writers years ago,
n episode. I was usually with
since he would always watch
tapings of his television plays or rehearsals of his stage plays, I got drafted whenever there was a shortage of actors. I was never any good, but I enjoyed getting involved in all these. The excitement was catching, and my family was thrilled whenever they saw me on television or read my name somewhere. Being married to a writer certainly pushed me into writing, particularly because he encouraged me constantly. Some of my poems were published, and we co-authored a short-lived television series once. But, I knew my limitations; besides, one writer in the family was enough.

Books dominate our lives, not only because he is a writer, but also because he is a professor of literature and critical theory. Our children grew up with books all over the house. One of our major considerations when we were looking for a new house was the amount of shelf space we could build in the empty spaces. We also needed a fourth bedroom that we could convert into a library. I have built shelves in the library, in the bedrooms, near the dining room, on every possible landing, but have refused categorically to put book shelves in the living room. He tells me that that space is the last frontier. We have resolved the problem of space for books—he has donated thousands of volumes to the De La Salle University Library.

HOW WE met and married is in itself an adventure. I first met him in July of 1969 when he was assigned to teach for a year or two at the Ateneo de Davao University. He was a Jesuit scholastic, while I was almost engaged to someone from Iligan. It could have been fate, because had I not gone home for some minor surgery, we would never have met.

I was teaching at the Mindanao State University in Iligan before we met, but I went home in October of 1968 because there was a cyst that needed excision. Coward that I was, I went home to my mother who, of course, made a lot of soothing noises and gladly took care of the bill. A few weeks' recuperation was needed, and by the time I was ready to go back, I was too late for the term. So, I found myself teaching at the Ateneo de Davao that term because one professor could not make it in time for the start of classes. After that term, my parents insisted that I stay home in Davao, which I did. It was, after all, quite advantageous to me. I paid no rent, the family car took me wherever I went, and my parents did not mind subsidizing my clothes. Plus, I had the comfort and security of being home. Life was sweet though uneventful.

When we first met on the football field, the sun was in my eyes and I could not see his features very well. I knew, however, that he was nice-looking, tall enough, and slim. He was with an older priest who introduced us. Before we actually met, professors and students alike were already talking about him. Brilliant, some people said. A genius, an accomplished priest, a man of many talents. The operative word, however, was "priest." Also, with a boyfriend tucked away somewhere, neither was I available. So I ignored him until we worked together on *West Side Story*.

When he presented a sneak preview of the school production of *West Side Story*, the faculty had mixed reactions. Mine was to volunteer to help in improving it. I thought that none of the cast could act, and their voices were too thin. Because he was a gentleman, he could not refuse the offer, although he did tell me later that he thought I was an interfering amateur. When he saw the results some weeks later, he was impressed and kept me on the team. By this time we had become friends, of sorts. He told me of his reservations about being a priest the rest of his life one evening while we were waiting for rehearsals to begin. The question he asked me was, "Do you think I'd make a good priest?" I retorted by saying that if he were not to become a priest, the alternative was to be someone's husband. So I asked him the question, "Do you think you'd make a good husband?" He said he did not know, but he was sure that as long as he had his typewriter, he would be happy. My answer? "Then be ready to cuddle up to your typewriter."

What did I see in him, and what did he see in me? Why did we like each other? We are not exactly compatible despite twenty-seven years of marriage. I was not thinking of compatibility the night he asked me to marry him as soon as his dispensation came through. After all, the physical attraction, the feeling of rightness about being together was quite strong.

A friend of mine told me months after my husband and I first met that when she met him, she thought he would be perfect for me. He was brilliant, he was accomplished, and he liked the arts. I was not accomplished, but I was considered intelligent. I also liked the arts very much. For instance, my family thought I was weird because I liked classical music when I was in high school and liked the opera when I was in college. I also read poetry and novels constantly. My saving grace was I knew how to dress with style, and could be

The Cruz family

quite daring at times. I was also a reckless devil, according to them. My childhood was fraught with adventures and mishaps. One of my brothers once tied me to the kitchen post to prevent me from going for a swim in the river near our house. I had a habit of jumping from the roof of our neighbor's boathouse into the river.

My husband, on the other hand, is paranoid. He is extra careful, always mindful of safety and having contingency plans. He will go to considerable lengths to ensure the safety of his things, such as wrapping books in plastic bags, all five thousand of them. He will not move from the sidewalk once a car that is several lengths away starts to back up for fear that the car would lose control and run him down. He will never think of climbing a tree to get a better view, or sitting on the balcony railing because he could fall down. He takes multiple doses of Vitamin C capsules the minute he sniffles. My children grew up with constant reminders of "Be careful." This sense of caution is the reason he packs an umbrella in his suitcase when he goes on an out-of-town trip.

He also has absolutely no dress sense. He buys the same style of shoes year after year, and his knowledge of color coordination is limited to the very basic. His children have threatened to disown him a number of times because he dresses oddly. I have told them that their father has no sense of style and that he only cares for comfort. His knowledge of fashion (or lack of it) borders on the funny. He once referred to Olga Cassini repeatedly in a conversation. He does not care for brand names, and he will not spend money on designer wear. But, he will not mind paying a small fortune for his computer, which he equips as lovingly as most men would equip their cars.

After all these years, some symbiosis has happened. We have acquired some of each other's likes and dislikes. I have managed to give him some awareness of fashion or style, simply because I give him clothes every chance I get. He is still unassuming, however, not given to small talk, and never assertive in public unless he was attending an academic forum.

He, on the other hand, has influenced my taste in literature somewhat. He has taught me to like the theater. I have succeeded in getting him to listen to classical music at home, but he draws the line at opera. He still falls asleep whenever I play an opera on the stereo or VHS. He has learned to like paintings, and he no longer laughs when he sees an odd sculpture. He used to think of architecture as the shape of a pile of bricks and stone. The few times we went on a tour, he could not understand why I would get so excited whenever I saw a particularly old building. This view changed only when he went to Oxford and saw the awe-inspiring architecture and interiors of some buildings there.

My husband's real gift to me is his view of the world. Although honesty and integrity have always been important to me, I never paid much attention to the sanctity of ideas and their free expression. Through his eyes, I have learned to appreciate the need to be more creative, more unorthodox in my thinking and more receptive to new possibilities. With his logical mind, I have been forced to re-examine my assumption and views about other people.

We may look like opposites on the outside, but where it matters we are very much alike. People usually think of us as opposites, and this is borne out by their remarks. For instance, very few people conclude automatically that I am his wife when we are together.

Years ago, I used to pick him up on certain nights from the university. I would knock on his door which opened into the main aisle of the largest building in the university. As I knocked on the door, I noticed a woman standing several meters away looking at me rather oddly. When I walked back to the entrance where she was standing, she turned out to be a friend of his who also knew me slightly. *"Ikaw pala,"* she said. "I was wondering who the glamorous woman was and since I thought that you could not be Isagani's wife (too glamorous), I figured you were knocking at Tony's (another university person who she thought was entitled to a glamorous wife) door.

I thought it was hilarious, but on hindsight, we do look like incompatibles if only appearances were considered. But, we value the same thing. His beliefs are mine, not because I should follow my husband, but because these are the same beliefs that I have had since childhood. I do draw the line, however, at some of his extremely liberal views. My occupation is different from his, and naturally my causes will not always be his. But his causes and principles will always be mine, because these transcend my mundane world and provide me with a view of what really matters.

If I have been the wind beneath his wings, he has always been my hero. He may be odd, unconventional, and will never cut a dashing figure or be a social success. But, his contribution to society and life in general will outlive the two of us. That is why writers will always be important; that is why he is important. And that is why I will continue to make life easier for him. And when we are old and doddering, we will look back and be content.

June Poticar Dalisay
The Early Years

I was twenty-three and was a full-time activist when I first met Butch. He was sitting in a corner busy drawing on a metal plate. Butch was tall and skinny then and his head appeared too large for his thin shoulders. I noticed he was chain-smoking. We were formally introduced at the office of the Printmakers Association of the Philippines (PAP) by Orlando Castillo, a mutual friend who was PAP president at that time. I knew he too was an activist because I would see him at the UP and in rallies and demonstrations. Butch was just released from Bicutan as a political detainee and was, therefore, unemployed. And to keep himself busy, he made prints which he would sell. We became friends and started exchanging notes and letters. At first, the letters were mostly about work and politics. Later, they became more tender and eventually became love letters. One day we discovered we were in love! I have kept the letters—written in Filipino. I don't think anybody writes that way now. They seem so corny and old-fashioned. Once in a while, when I get the chance, I'd read them and laugh.

Butch and Beng, 1986. In the background is a painting by Beng.

Ours was a whirlwind romance. I had known Butch only three months when he proposed. But before that we "courted" each other for a month or so and went steady without realizing it. Come to think of it—I don't remember Butch ever inviting me to a movie. Anyway, marriage was very far from my mind, so I was surprised when he informed me of his intentions over dinner at Skorpios Restaurant in Cubao. It was our favorite restaurant which is long gone now. Well, Butch was able to convince me that marrying him was the right thing to do. I believed him and said, "*Sige na nga.*" To this day, I kid Butch about his coercing me into accepting him. But I'm thankful he did. If he had done it much later, I would not have experienced the joy of motherhood and there wouldn't be a lovely, wonderful daughter named Demi.

Beng and only daughter, Demi

The next month, we were married at Manila City Hall. It was 15 January 1974— Butch's twentieth birthday. We made our own invitations. Butch wrote the text and I designed the card. There were around seventy invitations and we typed the text on each one. The rings we bought at La Elegancia for ₱150 each. Our wedding was a simple one since we couldn't afford and didn't believe in an expensive celebration. The reception, a merienda cena, was held at the Bungalow Restaurant. It was a buffet of native delicacies like *puto, pancit, fresh lumpia,* fresh fruits and coffee. What surprised us that afternoon was a small wedding cake which the restaurant staff gave us. Yes, we didn't plan on having a wedding cake because it was beyond our budget. The cake was small, but very lovely and could only be shared by about eight people. That very beautiful and touching gesture by the restaurant staff made our wedding a very memorable one. At this point, Butch was already employed as a writer for *Philippine Development Magazine*, a quarterly of the National Economic and Development Authority (NEDA). I eventually joined the NEDA in 1976 as layout artist after two years of being a full-time housewife.

As a young couple in the midseventies, we were contented with being husband and wife; Butch was happy being a young father to our only child. Weekends, we would bring Demi to the park, the carnival or to her grandparents' place. But most of the time we would just stay at home, watch TV, read some books and play with our daughter. So it was a more or less quiet and simple life: no complications, no challenges. Until one day, a news article came out in the papers announcing the annual literary contest sponsored by the Cultural Center of the Philippines. Butch thought he would try his luck and submitted a short story entitled "Agcalan Point," which was set in Romblon where he was born. I remember he showed me the draft for my comment, and I gave some suggestions here and there. I seldom do that now, simply because he never asks me to. The truth is, it would make me happy if he would. Well, I guess I'm more useful in other areas. Like, he says that it makes his work less stressful when I make him his coffee; or when I cook him his favorite *lugaw* or chicken macaroni soup. In short, he writes while I take care of the creative needs or sustenance—food to keep him awake and sharp.

"Agcalan Point" won. After his first successful attempt, there was no more stopping his joining contests. I guess I also encouraged him. Butch joined the CCP and Palanca Awards for Literature almost every year. He wrote mostly one- and three-act plays in English and Filipino and short stories in English. However, his serious interest in the past ten years has been fiction. Six books have seen print through the U.P. Press, Anvil, and Cacho Publishing. These stories were written in the Philippines, U.S.A. and Scotland.

BEING MARRIED to a writer like Butch requires a tremendous amount of patience and understanding, plus a superhuman effort to be emotionally and physically strong. Yes, it is difficult living with him. Living with him is like riding a swing which goes up and down. These ups and downs are the emotional highs and lows I experience and which eventually exhausts me. When this happens, I may become quiet and a bit irritable—like any other wife. When Butch notices this, he would try to cheer me up by cracking some corny jokes. But, of course, I always laugh. One of his favorite lines which pacifies me goes like this, "I know I'm grumpy but I love you." This is his way of saying, "I'm sorry," and gullible me would always accept such offering for the sake of peace and harmony.

Butch and I came to know each other intimately only after we were married. The first few years with him was a getting-to-know-you period. Little by little, I learned about his unknown side. For one, he was almost useless in the house. Being the first born, he was expected to excel in his studies and was not required to do much in the house. It is just his good luck that I can perform different tasks in the house and find joy and fulfillment at the same time. When Butch starts writing, another personality would emerge. *Suplado pala at masungit.* I tell him this and he only smiles and says, "That's why I married you."

My husband would always "announce" that he has some writing to do. This means that he requires silence and, if possible, have no distractions. Demi learned at an early age to accept and understand this need of her father. I would explain that her *Tatay* needed to finish a project, and off she would go to her grandparents, *titas* and *titos,* so she would have someone to play with. While the man of the house would be writing, I would busy myself with housework, gardening or painting. However, I would make sure that there is always food to dispel the monotony of writing. He consumes gallons of Coke and coffee when busy. These creative moments would make him so grumpy. But he wouldn't be Butch if he wasn't.

When the film director Lino Broka was still alive, he always requested Butch to do a script ASAP. This meant finishing a screen play usually in a week or two. Butch would pound away on his typewriter with such concentration he would forget to sleep.

Beng at work with her book designing.

The best I could do was to attend to his needs—a massage on the shoulders and neck helped a lot. Many won't believe this, but one time I had an out-of-body experience. It was late in the evening and Butch was rushing a screenplay which was to be submitted the next day, the day he was also scheduled to leave for the U.S. Elaine, Butch's younger sister, assisted him that night. But I was very tired, so I excused myself and went to bed. I didn't sleep right away because I was worried about Butch. Eventually, I drifted off to sleep. The next thing I knew, I was floating and passing through the bedroom door out to the dining room where Butch was working. I put my arms around him and released a warm and gentle energy to sustain him through the night. The next day, I told him about my experience. Since Butch is a skeptic, I don't think he really believed my story. After such projects in the past, Butch would come down with a fever. Now, developments in information technology have caught up with him. He uses a computer now to produce everything with ease and speed, thus he no longer gets sick afterwards.

It irritates my husband when he's busy and I talk to him. So I talk to him only when necessary. Otherwise, I would make myself "invisible" by doing things quietly. I paint, sketch or read. Sometimes, I leave him for a while and take a walk. But what is nice about my husband is that he always tries to make up for neglecting me. When we were in the U.S. for his graduate studies in the late eighties, he would volunteer to cook, wash the dishes, or even do the ironing when he was not very busy. If he had little cash to spare, he would bring me to a movie and later treat me to a simple dinner—usually a chicken dinner. We would usually do this during weekends. Aside from watching movies, one fun activity we used to do was to check out garage sales. Butch would wake up early to buy the morning paper and go over the classified ads. And after breakfast, we would throw some fruits and chocolate bars into our backpacks and off we would go. It was really fun since it brought out the child in us.

WHEN BUTCH won his first award in writing, I knew he was destined to be a writer. Discipline, passion, perseverance and belief in himself have shaped my husband's career. I have always encouraged him to write, but I never pushed him. He knows I will always support him in his creative endeavors. But there have been many sacrifices to make as wife, mother, and friend.

In 1983, we decided Butch should quit his job and go back to college to finish his studies. He had quit schooling in the early seventies to become a full-time activist. I was working with Sycip, Gorres, Velayo & Co. when he went back to the U.P. It was a difficult decision for Butch because it meant giving up a bright career in government. He was being groomed to be Director when he resigned from the NEDA. I knew that his going back to the U.P. was the right thing to do. But I was scared at the same time since it made me the breadwinner of our family. There were bills to pay—a two-room house in San Mateo, a second-hand Volkswagen, the life insurance, our daughter's education, his tuition, books, etc. But I had to be strong.

Butch and I planned our moves. All his income from writing (screenplays and teleplays) we put in the bank. We decided to give up some comforts and luxuries. There were fewer books to buy and a shorter grocery list. Shopping had to be done only when necessary. Gifts for friends and family members become smaller and cheaper. I also gave up buying leather shoes and settled for imitation leather. This was the period I learned to pray more often, and my prayer was for my family to be spared from any serious illness or accident. I wasn't aware that as months passed, the gray hair began to appear on my head.

Butch graduated cum laude in 1984 and the U.P. Department of English & Comparative Literature took him in as instructor. In 1986, he was awarded a scholarship by the Fulbright-Hayes Foundation and he left for Michigan to pursue his MFA. After graduation, Butch pursued his Ph.D. in Creative Writing at the University of Milwaukee-Wisconsin. I resigned from SGV and finally joined him in 1989 after a three-year separation.

At the launching of *Islands*, a book by Jaime Ayala Zobel, with Butch Dalisay as co-author.

THE FIRST few months after Butch left for the U.S. was a difficult period for me. The bed seemed larger and the bedroom bigger. I couldn't believe I was missing this husband of mine, a husband who was so *masungit*. But I did. I cried the first few nights, but after some time I got used to his absence. Butch called me long distance frequently. But we realized it was expensive, so we decided he would call Manila only twice a month. Oh, but the letters—the letters were very long. He would send me a letter once a week. I would send him a pack of letters written over a week. The letters from home were very important to Butch because it sustained him in some ways.

Demi, my work, and family kept me busy and sane. My art and my interest in esoteric knowledge and eastern philosophy also kept me company.

I followed Butch three years later when he was pursuing his Ph.D. in creative writing. We rented a three-and-a-half-by-five-and-a-half-meter studio-type apartment which had no dividers but had a toilet and a bath, and was furnished with a stove, a refrigerator and a heater. Living in this apartment was difficult because there wasn't enough space for both of us. There wasn't a room Butch could lock himself in, so we made the best of what we had. Butch would study in a little corner and write, while I would use the small dining table to paint and sketch. I did the cooking and ironing most of the time. Yes, it was feudal but I couldn't do the writing, could I?

We were together once again, and that made us very happy. But there was a problem. We could not survive on the salary he was receiving from the University as teaching assistant, so I had to work. I didn't mind working and thought it would be fun. But I could not find anything that would fit my qualifications. So I accepted a job as a deli clerk. It was a part-time job, four hours a day, at $2.15 an hour. I would wash pots, pans and dishes, chop vegetables for salads, bake cookies, prepare sandwiches, clean the windows, sweep the floor, clean tables, and throw out the garbage. It was very exhausting but I learned to accept and to find enjoyment in my work. I had to—in order to survive. I would come home very tired and Butch would notice this. He would volunteer to cook meals for us and, sometimes, he would even massage my back. However, when he was extremely busy, he excused himself. I took care of myself and heated his soup.

Butch learned to do other things aside from cooking. Where did he learn to cook? Well, during one summer break, Butch decided to work in a Chinese deli called Wokman. He took orders, prepared the

With Nick Joaquin, the Gonzalezes, and Andy Cruz, in Mabini Street, U.P.

food, washed the dishes, and cleaned the place. Oh, he was also the cashier. The other household chores he was good at were ironing and darning. He darns very well until now, and does it better than most women.

WE ARE two different people. He writes and is well read and is knowledgeable in so many things. I paint and I draw. I am a good cook, too. Butch is a skeptic and a pessimist. I am a Theosophist and an optimist. I love vegetables. Butch adores meat, especially beef. He is impatient. I am patient. I have to be. I love small and noisy children. Butch doesn't like noisy children around him. I enjoy viewing art exhibits. Butch is thrilled by visits to computer and electronic shops. I want to go ballroom dancing. Butch would rather watch the dancers. I've always wanted to try unusual and exotic cuisine. Butch is loyal to the cooks who prepares his favorite Filipino and Chinese dishes. Watching romantic comedies and dramas relaxes me. Butch is relaxed by suspense and violence. The more bloody the movie is, the better for him.

WHEN WE got married, we agreed to live by certain rules—to be honest and just to each other; to be open and willing to accept criticism, and, lastly, to correct our mistakes.

Twenty-three years have passed. There are many memories to look back to, memories which are happy, some sad and ugly, and painful, too. But these are memories which have strengthened us and made us realize certain truths in life. I have learned to accept the fact that my husband is a difficult person to live with. Will he ever change? I don't know. Whether he changes or not doesn't matter now. But it gives me such happiness knowing that I am the person who can nestle deep in the warmth of his affection.

Butch Dalisay today

We are more open to each other than ever before. We still write to each other—notes and short letters. I think this is a very nice way of showing one's affection and concern for a spouse. My heart still flutters like butterfly wings whenever I see a piece of paper on the kitchen table waiting for me. I know it'd be from him.

I see some gray in Butch. We are both wearing bifocals now. I've a wider waistline and Butch has a bigger paunch which he dislikes so much. We've been experiencing some aches and pains here and there—and we've begun to forget names and faces. We both are more health-conscious now. Every morning, I make sure we take our vitamin pills. Goodness, we are growing old! But, we're going through it with humor and good cheer. It's the best attitude there is.

Butch will continue to write. I'll paint and draw. I'll cook if he is busy, and we will sit down and enjoy a simple meal. He may wash the dishes and later go back to his writing, feeling happy and satisfied with his meat dish. I'll bring him his coffee. He'll smile and thank me. I'll go back to the kitchen, clean up and maybe have a cup of coffee, too.

Joy Viernes-Enriquez
A Never-Ending Tale

※⦅✿⦆※

I still believe that there should only be one writer in the family and in ours that one is Tony. My role is that of speaker of the house and I have at no time committed my tales to print, that Narita Gonzalez asked me to write about the some twenty-nine or so odd years of being Tony's wife and perhaps I take exception now and tell it all in print, a process more difficult even than telling it orally.

The summer of 1967 was like any other summer in idyllic Dumaguete; Silliman University has been the site of many writers workshops and this particular summer was no different. I was then working with the radio station DYSR as an announcer and among my duties was to co-ordinate our classical music programs. After graduating from the university's school of music, I continued to keep my ties with the school by teaching part-time and performing with the school group. It was convenient for me as our broadcast facilities occupied half of the Guy Hall building that housed the music school.

Joy and Tony after a Dumaguete church blessing.

Every year, since the start of the writers workshop, in 1962 or thereabouts, the Music School faculty and students would be asked by the late Dr. Edilberto Tiempo and his wife Edith to provide a musical soiree for the writers and the writing fellows. I have, as in the past, been always part of these musical soirees; with baritone Elmo Makil, whose raw talent, and vocal interpretation of John Donne's "Tiger, Tiger," already showed signs of a promising career in theater.

This summer then was no different. I met Tony in one of the parties at the Tiempos' house. Nothing monumental or earth-moving at that meeting. I was with my theater friends Eleanor Sardual (nee Funda), Nora Ausejo, Amiel Leonardia, Arturo Dionson, to mention a few, who were then with the English department of SU; and, of course, Raymond Llorca, who was editing SU's literary journal, *Sands and Coral*. Tony was one of the writing fellows for that year's workshop. I really didn't know the outcome of the sessions. Like any other workshops when they ended, everyone went home. Although in Tony's case, he opted to come back to Silliman to finish his schooling. He was offered by Dr. Ed Tiempo the Edna Chapman scholarship so he could continue his A.B. Creative Writing course.

I met him again in the company of my friends Eleanor and Amiel. Ely and I both stayed at the Faculty Ladies Home. Tony was a frequent visitor to our place. We circulated in the same company. I was involved in many of Amiel's theater productions. Somehow our paths would always cross. I cannot exactly remember now when he started dropping by the radio station and waiting to escort me home. I had several "live" programs in the evening or I would pre-tape some of my programs for the following day, especially those that were aired very early in the morning. Tony would usually sit on the steps of Guy Hall and wait until my program was over. I noticed he'd have in his hands a manuscript, which he said he was editing. I think it was the very early version of *The Ant Hill*. From the radio station we would go out for light snacks and over a bottle of coke and peanuts I'd read parts of his manuscripts and make comments on it for whatever it

Tony and the big fish

was worth. This pattern went on for several months.

In due time my colleagues started to notice the frequency of his visits. I became the center of jokes of my office mates and colleagues. I was going on thirty, considered to be one of the most eligible bachelorettes on campus, and had been paired off to several available guys, but to no avail; at DYSR, they considered me a "hopeless case."

Perhaps my being a musician drew and attracted me to people in the arts, and it was but natural that the company I had were also artists in their own respective fields. Tony, a newcomer to our group, was fairly well accepted. When he attended the writers workshop, he was already a published writer, and had some five years of writing. He had been published in the national papers, such as *Philippines Free Press, Weekly Graphic*, etc. So, his becoming a part of our crowd was natural. He was taking courses at the English department. Most of his time was taken up with class work. In the evenings when I was free, the group would go to a place called North Pole, our watering hole on a KKB (*kanya-kanyang bayad*) basis. Depending on our various states of inebriation we, Ely, Amiel, Eph Bejar and I, would be discussing the merits and demerits of movies showing at Park Theater, a local cinema, or about a book, or of the latest campus gossips. Tony was always with us.

Perhaps, it was through our constantly being together that the attraction developed. The feeling was mutual. It was because of this that the getting-to-know-you period was relatively short. By October 1967, only a few months after I had met him, he proposed marriage, a proposal which I accepted—no questions asked.

We had a civil wedding on the 27th of October, and the church blessing on November 10 at the SU church.

We opted for a quiet ceremony. The minister, the late Rev. Peter Raterta, his wife Nang Rose; Ely, Amiel and the church janitor, who opened the church and prepared the altar, were the only ones present. Tony and I wore ordinary street clothes. No hassle. None of the trimmings and worries that come with big church weddings, which, by the way, Tony's mother, Amparing, had wanted him to have, being the eldest and only son in a brood of three. I was myself an only child. My mother had died many years ago, my father had re-married a woman whom I wasn't in good terms with. A big church wedding was out of the question although my DYSR "family" would have wanted the wedding-trimmings for me.

Tony and I did it our way. We had juice and chocolate cake after the ceremony, and later in the afternoon we took a plane to Cebu City for a three-day honeymoon. Unlike the usual honeymoon, where the bride and the groom go off alone, our maid of honor, Ely, in a mock escapade, came with us. She wanted to shop in Cebu. In Cebu, we saw published in the *Philippines Free Press* Tony's short story "The Hummingbird", which he had been writing prior to our wedding. It was reason enough to celebrate, aside of course from the fact that we had just gotten married.

We settled in Dumaguete City. Our first home was a room at the Ebarles' house; Mrs. Ebarle was a professor at the University.

I will never forget our first Christmas together. I realized that going out with a writer and living with him twenty-four hours a day would reveal certain characteristics which, even to this day, I have to adjust to and accept as part of his being Antonio Enriquez. This I have learned: when he has an idea forming in his head and he has to write it, he doesn't remember or take particular attention whether it is Christmas, your birthday, or some special day, say Valentine's Day. One particular Christmas, for example, a few days before the 24th, he had been moody. While the rest of the world was getting ready to celebrate, he had started to pound on his Smith-Corona typewriter. Like any typical housewife I prepared a special meal for Christmas Eve. I went to SU church for the traditional Christmas cantata, where I participated as member of the Silliman church choir. Tony opted to stay home. Later in the evening when I got home, I was talking about the cantata and the special Yuletide presentations and decorations in the church and other interesting happenings there. All I got in reply were grunts and *ahs* from Tony.

After a while, realizing there was no way I could elicit a reply or even just a word from him, I sat at the table, ate by myself the special meal I had prepared, and went to bed. I must have cried myself to sleep.

When I got up the following morning, he was still at his typewriter. He must have taken a few breaks in between to take a bite, and then back to his typewriter he went. This pattern went on for several days until New Year's Eve. Well, the first day of January, at about 3:00 o'clock in the morning, he finished the story he was writing and he went out by himself to celebrate at the corner store near the Ebarles' house. He drank *tuba*—coconut wine. The story was "The Night I Cry." No metaphor meant for me nor had it anything to do with my night's crying.

That was our first year of marriage, can you imagine? Actually, not a year! Take four days or so to make it just two and a half months of our being married!

I didn't quite know what to make out of this, but it has certainly taught me valuable lessons in understanding a writer. "Oh, boy," I said to myself; "this is going to be quite a life ... and this is only the beginning."

The following years were spent in Dumaguete, I continued with my job at DYSR while Tony finished his creative writing course. He took a job with Dr. Vicente Sinco, at the Foundation University. He edited the school journal, the only thing he had to do. He had happily taken the job, for he'd be free from the burden of teaching and now would have time enough to write more stories.

Like any struggling writer, perhaps it was out of necessity, to augment whatever income we had from our salaries, that he wrote stories almost every week. This time, I didn't so much care about his moods and barometric tempers, maybe because I was also busy at work myself. He did remember Valentine's Day and gave me roses that year: so sweet of him! One thing with Tony, you don't expect him to be consistent with his actions. He does things when you least expect them; if you want him to do something, he won't do it despite all your crying, cajoling, or begging. I've learned through the years to accept this and the peace in the family has prevailed.

He was sending his stories to different magazines in Manila, and one of the dreaded letters we didn't look forward to receiving were the "rejection slips." I saw to it that I'd be the first to receive these letters, and my immediate reaction was to hide them from him. Weeks later he'd wonder aloud by saying, *"Por que nuay pa man sale di mio istoria?* —Why hasn't my story been published yet?" Then I'd tell him about the rejection slip and the manuscript that was returned.

(Above) The young Tony. (Right) Tony now with pigtail.

He would be crestfallen. His moodiness would persist for the next few days. He wouldn't touch his typewriter for some time. Then, I'd notice he would start writing again. Through this period, I'd stay in the background and not say anything. Might as well, for my being a radio announcer meant I talk all day to an unseen audience. The quiet in the house was a welcome respite for me.

However, when the P75 checks for his stories would arrive, it was time for us to splurge a bit. Tony's favorite way of splurging was buying me special imported chocolates. Or we'd go over to Dainty Soda Fountain and have ice cream and chocolate cake. Sometimes, Ely and Amiel would come over to help celebrate: Amiel would prepare his favorite spaghetti dinner, complete with Italian Chianti wine. Ely wouldn't want to be outdone—she'd also cook her barbecued hotdogs with pickles, mustard and catsup.

Tony loves to eat and he loves to prepare his favorite fried rice—the whole works—complete with shrimps and Chinese chorizo. I learned to bake, and cook: a skill which could have been there all along; but didn't have an outlet before. Being married to Tony honed my cooking skills.

Tony is a systematic person. He keeps a file of all his returned manuscripts. Once, however, and only once as long as I can remember, he, in frustration and anger, burnt all of over 200 pages of manuscripts, the first draft of what years later after starting out afresh turned out to become the novel *The Living and the Dead*.

He set aside all manuscripts for some time and much, much later returned to them and started working on them again. His patience is endless. He reworks, revises, edits. He creates new stories out of old ones. Often times, I wouldn't be able to recognize the final draft of a reworked story.

The pattern which we had set before we got married was carried over to our married life. I'd be the first reader of his works, a process which made me share with him the joys and pains of birthing a story.

Our only daughter Vanessa was born in March 1969, in Dumaguete. We progressed from a one-room affair to a two-bedroom apartment, just a stone's throw from Silliman U. Tony quit his job at Foundation University and moved to Silliman. The addition to our family was a welcome one. Tony was a doting father, even if he had wished for a son. In fact, he had prepared a name for the baby: Anton Vladimir, after the Christian names of his favorite Russian authors, Anton Chekhov and Vladimir Nabokov. This sort of became a joke the late Dr. Ed Tiempo was heard saying, in his inimitable British accent: "Tony, what if it's going to be a girl? She will have to be called Antonia Baldomera instead."

We had to think of a girl's name a few days before my expected date. And on March 10, two years after our marriage, our first child came, and we had a name for her—Vanessa.

Parenting came natural with Tony. We shared chores in taking care of the baby. He was so caring and concerned, quick to notice changes in the baby's temperature. Vanessa was prone to convulsions, even with a low-grade fever, so we were very concerned about her health.

Being a father might have diverted Tony's attention but certainly it didn't diminish his writing activity. The year Vanessa was born was also the year Tony won his first Don Carlos Palanca Memorial award for the short story "The Icon". It was also the year my father died. These transitions in our family added new dimensions and meaning to our lives.

We took a brief trip to Cagayan de Oro to see the property my father left me and also to attend to other concerns. We didn't stay very long in Cagayan, we had left Vanessa, then two-months old, in the care of a co-worker at the radio station—Celia Mamicpic, who later became her baptism godmother. We also had our jobs to consider.

Vanessa, unlike other children, was baptized two years after she was born. Violinist Gilopez Kabayao promised he was going to be her godfather and wanted to be present during the baptism, and since he was on his European and US tours with Corazon Pineda, who later became his wife, we had to wait. Finally, when he could make it —it was another summer. Our writer cousin Mig Enriquez ("*Nono*," as he is fondly called by us) was one of the writers workshop panelists that year. He was Vanessa's other *ninong*, with Edith Tiempo as *ninang*. The morning service at the SU church was most memorable; Gilopez and Corazon Pineda played "Meditation," from Thais, by Massenet, and later in the evening, in a gathering of close friends for dinner at the Tiempo's home in Piapi, they performed an intimate full violin and piano concert for all of us. *Manang* Punay, Gilopez' sister, came all the way from Manila to be with us for Vanessa's baptism.

Summers, the holiday breaks, were events we looked forward to. After that eventful first Christmas, Tony saw to it that we spent at least two weeks in Zamboanga City, particularly in Labuan, a fishing village 32 kms. northwest of Zamboanga City. The place figures prominently in many of his stories. We would go fishing: a favorite pastime of Tony's father Isidro, who at that time had just retired from being the city auditor of Basilan City, which was once a part of the district of Zamboanga City.

Papa "Sid," as we fondly called him (he passed away two years ago as I write this) joined us in all our fishing trips to Labuan. It was from him I learned the ropes. I learned also a lot of sea-lore, sea chanteys, songs of the sea, and the many tales of the fishing village of Labuan. He'd regale us with stories of supernatural beings, and of their family's unearthly, strange experiences in Labuan when they first settled there, ages ago, the first Christian settlers among the pagan Subanons. He'd tell us these stories while waiting for fish to bite.

On these occasions, I noticed how endless Tony's patience was; as I looked after our fishing lines, or watched him preparing the hooks and hand-lines in place, seeing to it that everything was ready and in exact order. He told us why.

"Once you're out at sea and the fish strikes, you won't have time to fix your hand-lines nor waste your time on unraveling knotted nylons. The fish only bites within certain periods, and if you don't take advantage of that they're gone before you know it, *phyyyttt*, and that's it. No more bites."

Our fishing trips to Labuan, were experiences which I found rewarding and at the same time revealing. I realized that there were many facets in Tony's character that went into the shaping of his being a writer. These constant revelations and my discovery of other attributes make life with Tony really worthwhile. (I think it's more of his own discovery to find I can be stubborn and hard-headed too.) Later, when he wrote the story "Dance a White Horse to Sleep" and which years later would become the basis of his novel *The Living and the Dead*, he used the same folklore about the family patriarch which Papa Sid loved to tell us. It was a difficult novel to write and I saw him struggle though this particular novel.

Our trips to Zamboanga City were also language-learning experiences for me. Tony had three spinster aunts who spoke little or no English at all, Visayan, or Tagalog but only Spanish and Chabacano. I found them fun to talk with; so, armed with whatever Spanish I had from my some 21 academic units, I'd spend hours talking to them and learning of the rich cultural heritage of Tony's family and of Zamboanga *la bella*. And years later I became quite fluent with Chabacano.

On the other hand, Tony knew very little of my family save perhaps of my close relatives whom he met later. He tried to learn to speak Visayan to no avail. After almost thirty years between Dumaguete and Cagayan de Oro, he still cannot quite communicate in straight Visayan, although he understands the nuances of the language.

Two years after Vanessa's birth, in 1971, Indiana University in Bloomington, USA, offered me the scholarship which was awarded me in 1967, and which had been put on hold because I'd gotten married. Tony encouraged me to go. Since we were not quite sure if the financial award was adequate for the three of us, Tony opted to stay with our two-year-old daughter in Dumaguete. He continued to teach at Silliman U. He also continued to write, in spite of the declaration of martial law in 1972. And the following year he won another Palanca Award for his short story "Spots on Their Wings," which was included in his first published collection of short stories, a small edition of some eight stories published in Dumaguete, by a writer-journalist friend, Bert Pontenilla. In an expanded version, the collection appeared as *Dance a White Horse to Sleep and Other Stories* some four years later, in 1977, in Australia.

Martial law years put on hold most of the creative writing activities in the country. To begin with, all the literary magazines—*Philippines Free Press, Weekly Graphic, The Nation*, etc.—had been ordered padlocked by the "benign dictator," the late President Ferdinand Marcos. Filipino writers like Tony found no outlet for their works. Much later though, he was able to publish his stories in Kerima Polotan-Tuvera's *Focus*, a magazine.

It was during this period that he turned to the novel, and spent more time rewriting and reworking his old stories. I came back from the US in early 1974. Tony had gone back to Zamboanga City with our daughter Vanessa, since the political atmosphere in Dumaguete was getting hotter. Silliman U was the last university to be re-opened after martial law was declared. I wanted to go back to DYSR and Silliman U but with the changes taking place, particularly in management, it was not such a good idea to do so. We decided to stay in Zamboanga instead and look for other jobs.

When the staunch anti-Marcos mayor of Zamboanga City, the late Cesar Climaco, heard that Tony, or "Nonito" as he is called by the family, was home, "Sar" as he was called by everyone, being the chairman of the Zamboanga State Normal College board of trustees, and a long-time admirer of Tony's work, immediately hired us. (Mayor Climaco was assassinated on November 14, 1984, and though the assassins are allegedly known, his murderers have remained scot-free to this day. In broad daylight and right in the middle of town, an eye witness, Patrolman Benjamin Arquiza, was liquidated a year after the mayor's assassination.) Tony reported for work the following day and resigned the next day. The thought of teaching Hiawatha, and Wordsworth didn't look too enticing to him. The ministry of information (MPI) was getting organized and Tony found himself with the newly organized information arm of the "new order." On the other hand, with my degree and teaching experience, I joined Zamboanga State College, now the Western Mindanao State University.

With our new jobs, an entirely different form of activity took place and Tony's writing took the backseat. This time, our Zamboanga sojourn wasn't much of the holidays we used to have since Zamboanga, in fact the South, was now a "war zone."

Having just arrived from the US, I experienced some culture shock. It was unnerving. The endless nights of fear and gun-fires at odd hours, of tanks rumbling and troops patrolling the streets in the middle of the night, of check points found all over the city, and of the omnipresent threats of grenades and bombs hurled at offices, shopping centers, and movie houses—all these frightened me. Vanessa was five years old when I came back. I was shocked to hear that she could identify different sounds of different types of guns being fired by God knows who—by our soldiers or by the MNLF rebels. Every helicopter that flew by signified dead bodies being brought back from the battlefield, victims of an ambuscade or an encounter with the Bangsa Moro rebels. These dead soldiers came either from the islands of Basilan, Jolo, Tawi-Tawi, Cotabato, or from the Zamboanga Peninsula area. It was terrible, and yet in some inexplicable way exciting after a peaceful stay in the States.

This time the tables were turned: Tony was now in media, while I became the teacher. But the reversal didn't deter me from becoming involved in media activities, particularly radio. Tony's area of coverage was Region 9—the Zamboanga peninsula, Basilan, Sulu, and

Tawi-Tawi. He did extensive travel to all these parts of Western Mindanao. Whenever I had the opportunity to travel with him, I would visit places of special interest to me like Tawi-Tawi, Jolo, and the Zamboangas. I would "arm" myself with a tape-recorder, camera and with my best foot forward, remnants of my radio years with DYSR, I would find myself with the "natives," listening to their songs and observing dances although a war was going on. Their tales, and practices of long ago, like their struggle for recognition and identity were being disrupted by the on-going fratricidal war. I was able to document all these, while Tony did his chores for MPI. Sometimes, he'd join me in my recordings. These activities further enhanced Tony's writing insights. In a small notebook, which he always carried around with him, he set down his observation of people's character and his description of places and events. Facial features and garments did not escape his eagle eyes.

From 1974 to 1979, we were criss-crossing Region 9's areas. Later we'd concentrate on the Subanen tribes in the Zamboanga peninsula. I was then on the lookout for a tribe I could concentrate on, to document their folklore in its entirety. I was worried by the tribe's reluctance to admit that they belong to the Subanen community. I saw the urgency of documenting their cultural heritage before it was totally forgotten by the tribe, especially by the young. In the fourteen or so years Tony was with the Ministry of Information, we would, or rather I'd find ways and means to tag along, particularly when the trips were in the Subanen areas. This way, I was able to gather satisfactory samplings of their folklore. Occasionally, when Tony had the time, he'd act as my photographer, a hobby with which he had adequate practice from our Dumaguete years. This Subanen research study would be carried on in later years, even after Tony's stint with MPI was over. He would also be making his own note-taking, particularly of events and happenings among the Subanens—particularly in Sindangan and Lapuyan areas. All these found their way into the making of the novel *Subanons* (this, he said, should be the way to spell it: the traditional way). The novel won him another Don Carlos Palanca Grand prize, with co-winner novelist Butch Dalisay, in 1993.

His years with the Ministry of Information also brought out certain facets in Tony's character, which was a revelation to us—Vanessa and me—as a father, a husband, and as a government man. He was designated as Assistant Regional Director for Region 9. His devotion and loyalty to his responsibilities took the upper hand. Sometimes we became second priority to him. We were always worried for his safety and well-being. There were days and nights that he wouldn't come home or inform us of his whereabouts, usually in places where "trouble was always broiling," as for instance in Jolo when it was burnt down by MNLF rebels; in Bongao, Tawi-Tawi, when MNLF rebels launched attacks within its perimeters, or in the stronghold of former MNLF commander, now governor of Basilan province, Gerry Salapuddin, in Sumisip, Basilan island. It was only after an event had taken place that we'd know about it and this was very much later.

During these years, Tony never thought of an 8:00 o'clock to 5:00 o'clock working sked. Maybe, because of the nature of his job his drinking became really bad, and he was also smoking excessively; two to two-and-a-half packs of Philip Morris daily. We were constantly worried about him. He no longer had time to write. The only significant work that came out during this period was his collection of short stories *Dance a White Horse to Sleep and Other Stories*. The stories which went into the collection were reworked or rewritten stories of earlier years. There wasn't one new story in the collection. University of Queensland Press, at the University of Queensland, Australia, published the collection as part of the Asia and Pacific Writing Series.

Occasionally, because of the trips he undertook to different parts of the region, he'd write feature stories for the newspapers or magazines; usually about the tribes he visited or some developmental ac-

Tony and grandson Julien

tivities. These were not literary pieces, but at least he was writing.

One of the projects that he concentrated on was the department's "cultural revival project." It meant the documentation and recording for the preservation of the cultural heritage of the various ethnic communities in the region. It also meant re-enacting and reliving traditional customs and practices of the people. This was most significant because there were groups that were fast losing their traditional practices in favor of more contemporary ones. The cultural revival project worked both ways, it awakened our own awareness of the rich cultural ethnic heritage of the South. In turn, it also made the lumads or tribal people, appreciate what they had and to realize that they must do something to preserve their cultural heritage for the future generation.

It was during these trips that I started to do a serious study on the Subanens, keeping detailed field notes and recordings of all the trips in the Zamboanga del Sur and Zamboanga del Norte areas. Tony also did his own note-taking.

Apart from the fact that he was really busy with his MPI job, he, almost always, took time out to read books and keep tab of latest publications here and abroad. Whatever time he had he would also take us out on our motorcycle, outings which we looked forward to.

He would sit at his typewriter and attempt at writing a literary piece—probably to no avail as I'd see crumpled or torn pieces of paper on the floor days later. It was also during this period that he tried reworking his old stories, some of which became part of a longer work, a novel, entitled *Surveyors of the Liguasan Marsh*, which he completed in Cagayan de Oro, during his "exile" there.

In the early '80s, our family moved to Cagayan de Oro. I should have been happy and would have welcomed the move, because I happen to be from this city. It was also an opportunity to renew childhood friendships and the retelling over and over of the (mis)adventures of childhood with childhood friend, Doring Roa, nee Ramiro, whose hubby Dondon could still hold us spellbound with his faultless Frank Sinatra voice with, the song, "My Way."

Tony, Joy, Julien, Narita and N.V.M. in Davao, with Aida Ford, at the latter's Ford Academy of Arts

But the circumstances behind our transfer wasn't a cause for celebration. Perhaps, Lawyer Reuben R. Canoy's observation would be apt for this portion of our lives. Attorney Canoy, or "Ben," as we fondly call him, was at one point in time the undersecretary of the Ministry of Public Information, with Senator Kit Tatad as head. Here is a part of the oral book review which Ben read during the launching of Tony's novel, *Surveyors of the Liguasan Marsh*, his second book with University of Queensland Press, the 16th in the Asia and Pacific Writing Series; and I quote:

"As a government information officer in his native Zamboanga, Tony became very unpopular with his [Manila] bosses for trying to expose a case of corruption. The crusade resulted in his transfer—or exile—to Cagayan de Oro where the system for which the present regime is well-known also operated with the same vengeance. Soon he found himself grounded or frozen.

"The enforced idleness was intended to shame Tony into resigning, but he decided to turn adversity to an advantage. It was during this period that he was able to complete the novel that we have come to celebrate.

"If we would only be sure that oppression invariably leads to a burst of creative activity on the part of writers, musicians and artists, I might be less inclined to disagree with the present order. But Tony's case, alas, is more the exception rather than the rule."

The following years were nightmarish for the family. Perhaps, it was our faith in God, our trust in each other, that kept our family intact and even brought us closer to each other.

Luckily, I found another job as a professor at the Philippine Studies Program at Xavier University, teaching folklore courses with the late Fr. Francisco R. Demetrio, S.J., then curator of the XU Museum de Oro.

Tony, because of the pressures and stress at the MPI, took a leave of absence. Fr. Ernesto O. Javier, S.J., then president of Xavier University, offered him a writer-in-residence post, which he had for a year or so. The break gave him time to take stock of the situation, gather his inner resources and strengths. It was also a good time to go back to his writing, and to reassemble his life, our lives.

It must have been very difficult for him. We, Vanessa, who was about 10 years old, and I, felt this inner turmoil. We had to cope with his moodiness, his barometric tempers; his desire to abandon his writing once and for all. Apart from this he was plagued by all kinds of illnesses. His throat was sore most of the time. His doctor advised him to stop smoking. Then the cases of beer diminished to bottles; and the late nights out became less frequent. But whether he could still write or not was another thing. And to watch him suffer was terrible for all of us. He would be lost in his own world and not come out of it for several days. Meanwhile, he would be very temperamental and moody. But he never was physically violent.

When he was in one of these moods, one activity he'd indulge in was to take apart either his typewriter or his motorcycle, a Honda XL-125. I recall, many years ago, one lazy Saturday afternoon, everyone was loafing outside the house and here was Tony moving around, restless. The next thing I knew, he got our motorcycle and started taking it apart: piece by piece—the tires, the seat, the screws, the nuts and bolts, etc. I usually have my line, but all I could say then was: "Mahal, are you sure you can put that back together?" Anyway, here were all the parts of what was once our motorcycle, laid out on the floor on sheets of newspapers. Our two-year-old Vanessa was circling around, picking up a nut or a bolt, asking his Papa what it was! Tony then cleaned with gasoline and oil every bit of the motorcycle parts. And now the task of putting it back together began! I held my breath—though I didn't show it to him. To add to my apprehension, I heard him muttering to himself: *"Donde caha yo el pone este?—* Where do I put this?"

By mid-afternoon our dis-assembled motorcycle started to take shape. The crucial thing was whether it would start again. He cranked the machine and, lo and behold, it did start and run too! Then holding up two-three pieces of nuts and bolts and screws, he said: "I wonder where these extra screws belong to?"

And so, as we traveled I kept my fingers crossed; that our Honda XL-125 would stay together in one piece. Afterwards, our motorcycle was dismantled so many times and successfully put back, that it didn't bother me any more.

I found out later it wasn't just our motorcyle that he dismantled but the typewriter and the electrical appliances (he's so adept at repairing them), and other things around the house that caught his fancy. I soon discovered that these taking-apart-putting-it-together binges occur when he has a story in mind and he's in the process of creating it, and the next phase is putting it down in writing.

After his Xavier University stint, due to some financial constraints, and other obligations, and with his leave-of-absence over, we had to decide, and found out that we hadn't much choice but for him to go back to his job with the information department. During his two-year-leave, the leadership had changed, from Francisco Tatad to NMPC's Greg Cendaña. Tony was recalled from Cagayan de Oro to the Zamboanga office. We'd more or less settled down in Cagayan de Oro. We had renovated my old ancestral home and turned it into a pension house and restaurant. We named it *Casa Hidalgo*, after Tony's pen name, "Hidalgo," in his Palanca Grand Prize winning entry *Surveyors of the Liguasan Marsh*. Part of the cash prize went to the mahogany main door and Spanish grill windows. Vanessa and I chose to stay in Cagayan de Oro. Furthermore, I was also quite settled with my job at the Museum de Oro and the Philippine Studies department at Xavier University.

With the change in leadership in Tony's office, there was also a shift in priorities. In the process some real good "cultural revival" programs were scrapped or revised, and the materials, like photos, slides, folklore, et cetera, which had, through the years, been collected in the earlier period of the information department were either discarded, or nowhere to be found. On Tony's first day in office, he found pictures and slides, smudged and wet, on the tiled floor of the office's comfort room. Such a waste of time and people's money!

Tony however stayed on with the department until the EDSA revolution of 1986, when Mrs. Corazon Aquino, through "people power," took over as president. A few months after she assumed office, those who had been working under the Marcos regime were asked to resign, particularly those occupying key positions in the regional offices and this included Tony. He chose to come home to Cagayan de Oro, even when they were re-hired the following day after they were "fired." Out of *delicadeza*, and although he had been designated officer-in-charge of both the MPI and NMPC regional offices, Tony chose not to go back. He saw this as an opportunity to concentrate on his writing: and that is exactly what he has done since then....

We have four grandchildren, two boys and two girls, one of whom is named Anton Vladimir. Tony had his wish finally fulfilled of naming a progeny after his two favorite Russian writers. They are all lovable imps who get in the way of his writing and test his patience.

Tony has written several books: three novels, *Surveyors of the Liguasan Marsh, The Living and The Dead,* and *Subanons;* four collection of short stories, *Spots on Their Wings, Dance a White Horse to Sleep, The Night I Cry and Other Stories,* and *The Unseen War and Other Tales.* He now uses the computer instead of a typewriter. I inherited his Olympia, since I can never get around to learn the commands of a PC. We own a jeepney. He uses the motorcycle occasionally to go hunting wild pigeons, since his interest has now shifted from the sea to the mountain. Tony's gray hair and receding hairline make our daughter Vanessa say, "Dad is HIV positive," meaning his "hair is vanishing." He complains of aching bones and muscles. Tony continues to spin his tales. Our partnership, the loving and caring in spite of all the odds, has endured the test of time and has flourished through all these years. We have, I noticed, mellowed. We are traveling less but the hunger for adventure is still there.

As mentioned earlier, we have maintained our ties with our Subanen friends and often visit them. These visits help in the translation, transcription, and clarification of the recorded materials which we had collected in earlier years. These materials are valuable documents of the products of human behavior. Tony beat me at writing the Subanen book. He came out with his own version, based in a true-to-life incident, the novel *Subanons.* In the near future I'll come out with my own folkloric version. This is no contradiction, really, to my saying that there will be only one writer in the family. But just you wait and see, I may succeed in becoming one!

Meanwhile, another novel is in the offing, a historical novel of Zamboanga, working title, *Zamboanga Odyssey.* It has become a family joke because although he has written over 600 pages, his hero is nowhere in sight yet. But after reading the first few chapters, I realized the magnitude and the many more months of work that he will have to put into this magnum opus, a work that he has been concentrating on for the last few years. I've assisted and joined him in the many, many years of research, in data gathering; in the fieldwork he'd undertaken in some areas of Zamboanga; in the endless interviews with people who know personalities who have contributed to the making of Zamboanga. It has taken him some five years to consolidate the materials for this first-ever attempt to write a historical novel about Zamboanga. He calls it the *Zamboanga Odyssey*. But whether this will be the final title, knowing Tony, only time will tell. Meanwhile, his growing immediate family and circle of friends support and prod him on.

Joy today

Tony has been translated in German and Korean languages; his stories have been included in anthologies and collections with other Filipino writers here and abroad. His works enjoy some degree of following, and some have become subjects for academic treatises. A novel which has been rejected twice for publication here in the country was eventually published in Australia and, surprisingly, is enjoying some degree of popularity. One of his novels has become a source of information by environmentalists, social scientists, and developers. I'm referring to his first Carlos Palanca Grand Prize winner, *Surveyors of the Liguasan Marsh*.

One of the activities that Tony enjoys most is joining writers workshops (it was, before, anathema to him, and usually he stayed clear of them) as a panelist. He finds it reinvigorating and refreshing. It is also one way of honing his writing skills especially when he interacts with younger writers, and hears their modern views of writing. He also reads what they write. I notice that he spends time talking to them, encouraging especially those budding writers.

God has blessed us with a network of writer friends whom we can turn to when the "going gets tough." Writing is a solitary world. Tony still has to be part of the "land of the living;" to face the world of realities, like boiling an egg for his grandson Anton, cooking noodles for Julien or putting the newest addition to his brood of grandchildren, Mique to sleep, to hug Nikka when she trips or hurts herself and to do other mundane chores.

A family friend and his occasional reviewer, Mike Baños, in a book review he wrote for Tony's latest collection of short stories, *The Unseen War and Other Tales of Mindanao* says of Tony, the writer:

"Whether we have seen the best that's yet to come only time will tell, and like *bahalina* mellowing in their earthen jugs 'neath the cool earth, we are willing to bide our time until the season is ripe, that we may once more gather friends at a camp fire in the cool evenings of the boondocks of Mindanao and pour a glass of vintage Antonio Enriquez like this one round to warm our lost yesterdays."

And so, my life with Tony goes on....

This is our never-ending tale.

Narita Manuel Gonzalez
Our Life on File

E very time I get a chance (and there have been quite a few) I tell about how it happened that were it not for the late U.P. President Salvador P. Lopez, I would not have met N.V.M.

It was late one afternoon, in 1939, that we had a party in S.P.'s honor. By we, I mean the U.P. Literary Guild, the president of which was Alfredo Ag. Muñoz. Among our officers were Vesta Borbon and Victoria Fargas. I was treasurer. Being also an H.E. major, I had been assigned to bake the cake. On it I emblazoned in green icing "Welcome."

The tea party, which we held at the U.P. Social Hall, on Isaac Peral St. (now United Nations Avenue), drew quite a crowd. From the Manila journalistic community came Pura Santillan Castrence,

N.V.M., Narita and children Ibarra, Selma, Myke and Lakshmi

who, besides teaching at U.P., was a practicing columnist of *Manila Daily Bulletin*; there was Estrella D. Alfon, then just starting out and attracting much attention because of her Cebu stories. From the U.P. Writer's Club, a rather exclusive organization (you had to be invited to join the group) came several who were to become well-known in later years: Antonio Gabila, Renato Constantino, Lilia Villa, Caridad Guidote, Sammy Rodriguez, Simeon del Rosario, Juanito Quesada, and Marion Celi. Quite a few of those present then, like our guest of honor himself, and Estrella Alfon, could be exchanging stories with the patron saint of writers, Saint Francis de Sales: D. Paulo Dizon, Teodoro Lansang, Jimena Austria, Stevan Javellana, and Elizabeth Marcos.

But it was a fateful afternoon in more ways than one; very much in person was N.V.M. Gonzalez. He must have come with yet another writer's group, The Veronicans. Many of them were non-U.P. students and were known to us as "porch lizards." Their favorite hang out was Rizal Hall Square.

I never knew whether N.V.M. had been impressed by the fact that I was an officer of the Literary Guild or that I knew how to bake a cake, but after the party he took me home to Vermont St., where we lived, not minding the company of two friends of mine. This started a long friendship that involved books and, now and then, a few bars of Almond Joy, my favorite brand of chocolate. I was wearing somebody's military ring but that did not deter him. He became a very good and loyal friend.

In the second semester of 1941, I took graduate courses in English. In one class, we had Nelly X. Burgos for instructor, and she discussed a new novel, *The Winds of April*, the author being a certain N.V.M. Gonzalez. I was too shy to tell Miss Burgos that the author was a good friend of mine, that he might dedicate the book to me. He had entered the book in the Commonwealth Literary Contest, and he had invited me to the awards night. I had come properly chaperoned by a cousin. Juan C. Laya won first prize for *His Native Soil*, while

The Winds of April won honorable mention. As it turned out, it was to his grandparents that N.V.M. dedicated the book.

When World War II came and Manila was declared an open city, my father decided that we evacuate to Binangonan, in Rizal province. Every Saturday, N.V.M. came to visit. He took a *caretella* from Manila, changing rides eight times to reach Binangonan. The trip took four hours each way.

Eight months of Binangonan seemed all that the family could take. Our resources were dwindling, Father announced. The war seemed not to end. We must move on, he said, this time to La Paz, San Narciso, in Zambales province. This had been home to my parents.

The proposed move forced N.V.M. to make a decision. He could not visit us in Zambales with any kind of regularity. That August, he asked my parents for my hand.

"*Buotan man,*" my father said. He had known N.V.M. for three years. Mother agreed to Father's assessment. But she asked him, "How will you manage?" He was the sole earner in his family, my mother knew.

"We will manage." N.V.M.'s answer was in the vernacular, and he had used the word *maneho*, which sounded frightfully ominous. "You don't intend to be driving a taxi or a truck for a living, do you?"

We all had a good laugh over that afterwards.

In any event, N.V.M. was confident that his job as action clerk at National Coconut Corporation could see us through. For an engagement ring, he gave me a simple, thin band (it was said to be white gold!) that he bought with his first royalties from the novel.

We were married at Singalong Church. We were to learn later that the Capuchin priest who officiated, as well as our wedding sponsor, Mrs. Mariano Garchitorena, were among those killed by the Japanese who had literally put into effect their dreaded scorched earth policy.

It was during the Japanese Occupation that N.V.M. wrote in

Tagalog. He entered his short story *"Lunsod, Nayon at Dagat-Dagatan"* in *Liwayway* magazine, which then, even as now, was one of the most widely read periodicals in the country. At this point of time, it must be noted, no other magazine had been licensed by the Japanese authorities to publish. N.V.M.'s story won honorable mention, Liwayway Arceo's (*"Uhaw ang Tigang na Lupa"*) second prize, and Narciso G. Reyes' (*"Lupang Tinubuan"*) first.

N.V.M. receives from President Fidel Ramos the National Artist for Literature, 1997

After my father-in-law was released from Fort Santiago, we heard rumors that N.V.M. would be picked up next. The scare was so real that we decided to evacuate to Mindoro immediately. Our son was six months old by this time and every day counted.

We sold Mama Paz' piano, N.V.M.'s *Harvard Classics* and other books. I had a box of "Pablum" and a bar of "Lux" soap and many clothes and linen.

It was not easy at all to find transportation to Mindoro. We did finally hire a two-masted sailboat, a *batel*. Wonder of wonders, it took us two weeks altogether to reach a place called Paclasan, in southern Mindoro. Only there was yet some walking to do, a five kilometer stretch of beach to the barrio called Wasig.

We stayed in Wasig for more than two years. It was something of a forced vacation. We did not go hungry at all. Bananas by the bunches were always ripening near the open stone stoves. There was boiled *saba*, fried *saba*, or the *lupac*, boiled *saba* pounded with sugar and grated coconut meat. I had to learn to like goat's meat. Papa Vente had a herd and one goat was butchered now and then. I like best the goat jerky, *tapa*, very dry and fried crisp.

My little boy did not lack for clothes. I made him shorts or jumpers from my clothes. I even made a shirt for N.V.M. using a loose balloony dress.

The one bar of soap, Lux, I brought from Manila, lasted a year; it had served for the boys' use only.

For money to buy kerosene, laundry soap, etc. we sold coconut oil. Everyone in the family had to shred coconut. I was a very poor shredder. I took care of the baby and exempted myself from this chore. Papa Vente devised a coconut meat presser that could press a bigger volume of shredded coconut meat at a time. The pressed coco milk was cooked in a *kawali*. At first the *latik* was fun to eat. Afterwards it left a satiating taste with *malagquit* or rice and shredded *panocha*.

We were never harassed by the Japanese soldiers or rogue guerilla bands. A group of guerillas did come by one afternoon as N.V.M. was typing away in the shade of a coconut tree. The leader had come to commandeer the typewriter. How N.V.M was able to talk the leader out of getting the machine remains a miracle to this day.

N.V.M. managed to do some writing and fishing at this time. For my part, I discovered I could catch up on my reading. I was becoming heavy with child, our second, and I could balance on my tummy such heavy books as *And Quiet Flows the Don* by Mikhail Sholokov and *The Thibaults* by Roger Martin du Gard. I read a great deal of Hemingway and Chekhov, too. The truth is, I could not have read as much had I not married N.V.M. To this day, he still has this habit of saying, "Read this!" or "*Bah,* why bother with Danielle Steele?" Lately, he's been urging me to read Henry William Scott's *Barangay*—yes, the late Scottie, who had been our son Mike's friend. Our second child was a girl, and we called her Anselma, our Mangyan Princess.

We returned to Manila and found it devastated. We found a

crummy apartment in San Andres Bukid. Luckily, neither the retreating Japanese nor the avenging Americans bothered with this backwoods subdivision.

We had our third child, Michael. The hand-to-mouth existence that one often reads about became for us a reality, this especially when our ration of rice, bananas, meat and dried fish from the province failed to arrive regularly. But there were some breakthroughs: N.V.M. found a job as editor of *Evening News Magazine*, and he worked with a staff which included Mabini Rey Centeno and Carmen Guerrero Cruz-Nakpil, the Chitang who was so admirably chic then as now.

In 1949, N.V.M. won a study grant. He attributed this to *Seven Hills Away*, a collection of his stories which had just been published by Alan Swallow, in Denver, Colorado. The book, he believed, must have suggested to Dr. Charles B. Fahs of Rockefeller Foundation that exposure to American writing and writers would benefit him.

N.V.M. chose to go to Stanford, not to obtain a degree but to take courses from one of his favorite American writers, Wallace Stegner. Another favorite writer of his, Katherine Ann Porter, was teaching in Stanford, too, that year. From Stanford, N.V.M. went East, stopping at Lawrence, Kansas and then on to Gambier, Ohio, where he studied at Kenyon School of English. That summer took him to Breadloaf, at Middlebury College, in Vermont; and in the fall, he went to Columbia. It was a dream study program; he took only the courses he liked but did not earn a degree.

I stayed behind in San Andres Bukid with three small children. To the small pension which came with the fellowship I added the few pesos I earned by taking in sewing for the ladies in the American Embassy community. This was arranged for me by Mrs. Alfredo Morales in whose home the Women's Forum was organized. Among the members were Ruth Lava, Mrs. Jesus Lava, Flora Celi Lansang, Lydia Arguilla, an American lady surnamed Mercado, and others. Celia Mariano and William Pomeroy also attended the meetings. Celia, in particular, thought I would make a good member of some other organization they were talking a great deal about at that time. I was naive about Women's Forum; they were discussing current affairs that touched on issues relating to America and there was my husband away in the States at this time. In any case, the Women's Forum was the first cause-oriented women's group of the day.

When N.V.M. returned home from his study grant he taught creative writing at P.W.U. and U.S.T. Neal Cruz, Johnny Gatbonton, Ophelia Dimalanta and Arnold Moss were among his first students at U.S.T.

Meeting Nena Zumel just recently, I learned a little more about N.V.M.'s days at U.S.T. Nena, who was studying music and philosophy then, took interest in N.V.M.'s courses and took all of them. He should have stayed longer on the faculty there, Nena thought. Their class felt "orphaned" when he left. He had even succeeded in teaching *Madame Bovary* which was a no-no in U.S.T.

Today, N.V.M. occasionally sees his many U.S.T. friends at Mauro Malang's West Studio. They call themselves the Thursday Group, which includes, besides N.V.M.'s former U.S.T. students, along with those who also studied with him at U.P., principally Andres Cristobal Cruz and Rony Diaz. Also a Thursday Club member is another former student who came to the U.P. when N.V.M. was abroad teaching; he is the editorial writer, playwright and award-winning short-story writer Jose F. Dalisay. He

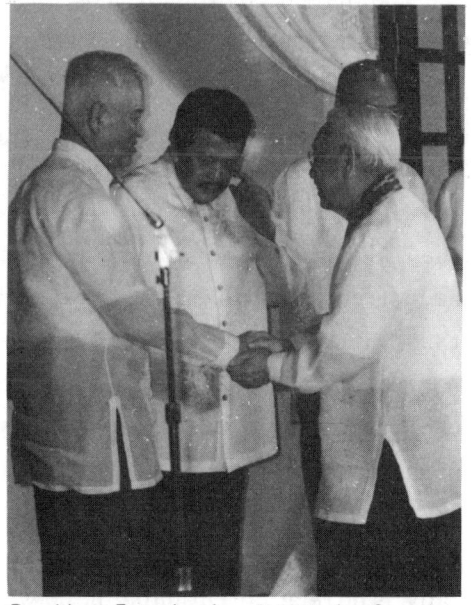

President Estrada gives N.V.M. the Gawad Sentenaryo 1898-1998 Artista ng Bayan sa Panitikan.

is often at the Club with his wife Beng, a water-colorist and the book designer responsible for one of N.V.M.'s latest collection of essays, *Work on the Mountain*. The cover features, in four colors, a photograph of a huge block of marble, taken in Romblon, the home province of both "Butch" Dalisay and N.V.M. Ajit Rye has been a recent addition to this Thursday Group.

His former students at P.W.U. are our good friends to this day. There is Dolly Benigno Acasio, who we discovered was a Bay Area resident at the same time we lived there; there's Ceres Santos C. Alabado, a pioneer in children's literature. Long an advocate for not only the writing of, but for the publishing of children's books and to the maintenance of a library especially for children, Ceres had founded PAMANA. She is a *comadre* and has moved to California, where she has now made her home. Another P.W.U. alumna is writer and editor Luning Bonifacio Ira; she and her writer-daughter Vanessa, who is currently in New York, an intern in that city's publishing industry. They have been two of the most professionally active of our writer-friends. Incidentally, Luning's husband, Rene, and N.V.M. have enjoyed some musical evenings together, doing piano and violin duets when the mood moves them.

To supplement his salary from teaching, N.V.M. once took a job with U.S.I.S., whose offices then were on Dewey Boulevard, in the U.S. Embassy Compound. He quit it early, though. The office set up a coffee bar that observed a "No Filipinos Allowed" rule, and that did it!

In 1951, Dr. Alfredo T. Morales, then Dean of the U.P. College of Education, suggested that N.V.M. apply at U.P. Some powers-that-be objected to this since N.V.M. did not have a college degree. But others thought that that need not be an obstacle. Enthusiastically behind the idea had been President Bienvenido Gonzalez who, incidentally, is no relation. Of similar mind was Professor Cristino Jamias, chair of the English Department. Subsequently, N.V.M. was appointed assistant professor. It was a rank he held for eighteen years until he left to teach in the States, on the invitation of the University of California at Santa Barbara. His U.P. salary had been pegged at P1800 a month, and he had been warned that whoever joined the university should be prepared to observe a vow of poverty.

Why didn't N.V.M. obtain a college degree? His having taught at five U.S. universities as well as at University of Hong Kong, and having been a college drop-out besides, did not make him a good example to his grandchildren, given the value that our society gives to educational attainment.

The fact, however, is that he had been a junior at Manila Law College and, on top of that, a classmate of his father. Although it came late in his life, the latter earned a law degree and practiced the profession. It is told in the family that one evening, in a class in criminal law, their professor called on N.V.M. He had not been listening to the lectures. He had in fact been writing a poem and couldn't come up with an answer to the professor's question. It seems that it was at this point that N.V.M. decided to quit school altogether. His classmate and father did go through with the course; he in fact passed the bar. N.V.M. carried on with his free-lancing, contributing to the Manila papers. Ironically, he gravitated to teaching in our universities—the U.S.T., P.W.U., and U.P.

The appointment to the U.P. faculty entitled him to campus housing. One unit of a duplex made of *sawali* was assigned to us in Area Two in 1951. It was here, as Professor Elmer Ordoñez was to note years later, that the first U.P. writer's workshop was held. Elmer's recollection had been quite remarkable: he named Virginia Moreno, Rony Diaz, Andy Cruz, Raul Ingles, Maro Sta. Romana, Alex Hufana, Petronilo Daroy, and S.V. Epistola as the first creative writing students at U.P. Tita Lacambra and Florlinda Soto joined the group later, as did Ramon Portugal who, at this time, was already with the U.P. administration.

When President Bienvenido Tan took office in the early fifties, he allowed the building of faculty homes on campus, restricting ownership only to the structures. Eighteen such homes exist to this day and are called "Pioneer Homes." It was in 1953 that we moved to one of these structures, P-11, located on Auxiliary Road, in the heart of Area One. The "P" in our address stood for "permanent." When, later, street names became Filipinized, our address became 57 Mabini St., Area One. A baby girl was added to the family at this new address, and we named her Lakshmi, a name we chose after our India trip in the summer of 1952.

One day, Eva Kalaw and Nina Puyat came to our house to tell N.V.M. that he had won the Republic Pro Patria Award. This was the first time that the award was being given. It was to be accompanied with a cash gift of three thousand pesos. The amount could not be raised, however, and the prize money was reduced to a thousand pesos. The money and the medal made us very happy nonetheless.

In spite of his heavy teaching load and seeing through the publication of *The Diliman Review*, which N.V.M. began for the College of Arts and Letters under the strong sponsorship of Dean Tomas Fonacier and Professor Cristino Jamias, chair for English, he continued to give workshops to groups outside the department. One such group was organized by Johnny Ramos, who was then finishing his music degree. He later became dean of the College of Music. Math majors joined enthusiastically and the meetings were held at home on Tuesdays. Grace de la Costa Lauzon, whom I met recently at Odette Alcantara's birthday party for S.V. Epistola, tells me that in that group Johnny Ramos put together had been Elmy Peralta, Rica Panganiban, Roly Danao, and Ed Escultura. We had a brief reunion with Roly Danao in Berkeley not too many years ago.

Throughout that time we lived in San Andres, moved to Mindoro, and then returned to Manila, N.V.M. did his writing in long hand, but later began to use a typewriter. He'd be at his writing just as soon as he was home from work. One of the kids would bring in his slippers, another his pipe and tobacco. He'd pound away at his typewriter quietly for a while, taking a break only to puff his pipe. Or he'd dally longer and play his violin. We left him very much to himself in the porch, where he liked to do his work. He finished *A Season of Grace* and *The Bamboo Dancers* this way. He had a butterfly chair that he was fond of, and it exists to this day. N.V.M.'s writing was now being much slowed down by his teaching and by his efforts to open for writers more outlets for their work. One of these projects was *The Diliman Review*, earlier mentioned. It answered the need for a creative arts program in the College of Liberal Arts, and a maiden issue was out January 1953 at two pesos per copy. The *Review* is still on-going to this day.

At some point, the Philippine Writer's League, of which Federico Mangahas was president, had become inactive. Another writer's organization could be useful on the scene. This was how the Philippine Writer's Association came into being with N.V.M. as president. He was able to obtain a grant of five thousand pesos, to be used as a revolving fund for the editing and publication of a collection of short stories. This was how *Katha I* came about. N.V.M. resigned as president when a new board of directors got elected and salaries and honoraria were paid for the earlier project. At first the publication of a *Katha II* was in jeopardy, but luckily, new financial assistance was found and the volume came out.

N.V.M. and Narita celebrate their 50th wedding anniversary.

N.V.M. observed that Benipayo Press had been publishing books in Tagalog for some time and he wondered why the same could not be done for English. Alberto Benipayo, who ran the family press, agreed it might be worth trying if N.V.M. helped in the selection of titles to be published, as well as in the editing and production. It was under this pioneering program that Bienvenido N. Santos' *You Lovely People* saw print. Other books followed: Gilda Cordero Fernando's *Butcher, Baker, and Candlestick Maker*, Gregorio C. Brillantes' *Distance to Andromeda*, Aida Rivera Ford's *Love in the Cornstacks*. For his pioneering intervention in the publishing of literary works in English, Bert Benipayo received an award. You would think that a new day had dawned for Philippine writing then, but the situation has remained rather as bleak as in the past. Poetry and fiction found their way in anthologies without permission from their respective authors, and although these books were repeatedly printed, their authors never received compensation for their work.

One day, Delfin Ferrer Gamboa, a short story writer and advertising account executive, sought out N.V.M. at U.P. They had a brief chat at the steps of Palma Hall concerning plans for literary prizes under the sponsorship of La Tondeña, a rum manufacturing firm. Among other things, they discussed entry rules, deadlines and the name for the awards. Delfin Ferrer Gamboa thought of calling the prizes La Tondeña Awards. N.V.M. felt that it would be so much better if the awards carried directly the name of the Palanca family. This seems to be the story of how the Palanca prizes got named that way. As one Manila columnist had remarked, it does sound better to hear "How many Palancas have you had?" rather than "How many La Tondeñas?"

The family had a real break in 1964. N.V.M. was awarded a research and writing grant with residence in Rome. This was godsend because our youngest daughter had been asthmatic and needed a change of weather, the doctor said. The grant was very modest, though. We decided to go for broke. We sold our piano and were among the first clients of a bank's lending program called "Fly Now, Pay Later." Things turned out well; our daughter's health improved. But we had to continue paying for the air fares for over a year and a half even after our return to Manila.

While in Rome, N.V.M. met Ed Loomis, a classmate of his at Stanford. He invited N.V.M. to join him at University of California, Santa Barbara as he was appointed chair of the English department. This was how N.V.M. found himself in Santa Barbara in 1968. He taught there for a year. Another classmate from Stanford, Robert Williams, invited N.V.M. to Hayward, and there he moved the following year. And that's where N.V.M. taught for eighteen years straight through, broken only by a year as visiting professor at University of Washington, in Seattle, and another year at U.C.L.A., in Los Angeles. For three summers, he also taught at University of California, Berkeley. As assets in academe, it has turned out, one's classmates proved to be greater than academic degrees. Incidentally, N.V.M. received an award in 1972 as "Outstanding Educator in America." But he did not have the thirty dollars to cover the price of the "award book."

Whether due to age or as the price to pay for teaching foreign students, N.V.M. developed hypertension and gout. To relieve some tension, he started making classical guitars. He finished four of these, one of which went as a wedding gift to our second son, Mike, who married Patricia Araneta.

After living in a condo for five years, we decided to sell it to our daughter. We bought a small house with a big yard. N.V.M. had a room of his own, and I had a space for an apple tree, nectarine, loquats, plums, and grapes. During summers, the scent of apples was pretty strong. I succeeded in planting *camote* and *chayote*, too. Thus we had *chayote* for chicken *tinola* and *camote* tops for salad. Quite a number of our Filipino friends had planted *chayote* likewise, and our vegetable rotted on the ground.

N.V.M. retired from California State University, Hayward, as emeritus professor of English. Now he could write more articles and short stories. I like the articles better than stories. His workroom was getting to look like that of Jose Garcia Villa's, according to Andy Cruz who, one day, turned up in Hayward. He had just visited Villa in New York, he said. Villa's room was littered with books and manuscripts; these were to be found all over. You had to try to keep from stepping on the piles of magazines, books, and manuscripts on the floor.

When I begin to tidy up N.V.M.'s room, he'd say: "Please don't touch anything. I know where to locate what I need." But when he couldn't locate a book in all that mess, he'd go and buy a duplicate. I do not know how many Susanne K. Langers we have had, how many Micrea Eliades, or how many R.K. Narayans there are in our library. These purchases of duplicates did not only involve books but envelopes, paper clips, and rubber bands, even music sheets, and scores for violin and guitar. The Asian American Center at U.C.L.A. has offered to collect N.V.M.'s old manuscripts, files and clippings. He's still thinking it over.

It was in 1987 that a great honor was given him by the U.P. In a ceremony at Abelardo Hall, N.V.M. received the Doctor of Humane Letters, *honoris causa*. Now, N.V.M. has a degree! Chancellor Ernesto Tabujara, who at the time was Officer-in-Charge, made the academic ceremony especially memorable for N.V.M.

We came home to U.P. to celebrate our 50th wedding anniversary. The mass was concelebrated with Jaime Cardinal Sin as main celebrant. We were happy and honored to have other Jesuits join him: Fr. Joaquin Bernas, Fr. Bienvenido F. Nebres, Fr. Nick Cruz, Fr. Joseph O'Brien, Fr. Joey de Leon, Fr. Art Ferrer and our own son, Fr. Nim. To assist the Cardinal were Msgr. Josefino Ramirez, rector of the Shrine of Mary Queen of Peace, Edsa. And of course, there was Fr. Pat H. Lim, a family friend of many years, and it was at his church, the Santa Maria della Strada, where the mass was held.

It was at the Della Strada Hall where we had the reception. "A marriage made in heaven?" Oh, my gosh! What a big order!—this was Belinda Olivares Cunanan's pronouncement upon us. How could we disappoint her? She had been one of N.V.M.'s earliest students at U.P. The last time we saw her was at her home, where she invited us for lunch. She and Thelmo had just been married then, and that was over thirty years ago. She had become a respected columnist of the *Philippine Daily Inquirer*. In the course of time, she has become a friend to countless people in government and business, and we had lost contact with her. How did she get wind of our celebration? Through none other than a mutual friend also that of the family and one of long standing. Belinda received an "order to attend" from Sister Pin Constantino, now a Carmelite nun, and an earlier colleague of N.V.M. at the University. This was how Belinda learned about the anniversary celebration.

The blessings continue. The University of Washington, at Seattle, published *The Bread of Salt* just about this time. By special arrangement a U.P. Press edition was issued. This made the book ever so much more available, as the American edition was rather expensive. A first book launching was held at the Philippine Consulate in Los Angeles, the event coinciding with a convention of Philippine and American scholars in the U.S.A. A second launching followed, this time under the auspices of the Center for Philippine Studies at California State University, Hayward. N.V.M. gave readings from the book, the tour taking us to Kansas City, Chicago, Washington, D.C., New York, Eugene, Or., and Seattle. It was not so much a book tour as a discovery tour, for it provided us with a considerable knowledge about how well our countrymen and women have been doing in various parts of the United States.

In an amazing way, the book tour became occasions for happy reunions. Our hosts in Kansas City were Dr. Lilian G. Pardo and Dr. Leopoldo Pardo, Jr., and what a welcome they gave us. It turned out that N.V.M. had been Lilian's instructor in a freshman English course at U.P. This was so many years ago; he had completely forgotten it. Lilian had not, and for good reason: she had received a low mark for the course. As a result, she shifted from English to medicine. Nonong Pardo remarked, "You should be glad about that grade! That was one English major less." But the Filipino community in America, we might add, had one more outstanding Filipino doctor, and destined, besides, to become the first Filipino president of the American Women Physicians Association. In Chicago, Chit and Danny Davila, and the de la Fuentes, who were medical doctors both, hosted us. The Avilas are old friends of the Pardos. In nearby Evanston, we discovered a Romblon connection in the doctors de la Fuente, the lady of the house being from Romblon, which is N.V.M.'s birthplace.

And who would also be in Chicago but Maria Luisa Aguilar Cariño, our Baguio poet and essayist, on her Ph.D. program at the University of Illinois? She arranged for a reading by N.V.M. at her department, and it was a great success. Luisa's dean sent N.V.M. a note of thanks that could be our pride and honor to keep. A dean, indeed, in so expressive and warm gesture of appreciation for both Luisa and N.V.M., Filipinos both, one young and the other not so young; this moved me immensely.

Then, off to Washington, D.C., where arrangements had been made for N.V.M. to speak at a convention. Dr. Jean Paul Dumont, who has lived and written about Siquijor island, in the Visayas, had us for guests. He and his wife had a flat crammed with books, not the least among them a set of the famous and now rare Blair and Robertson's *The Philippine Islands*.

Dr. Rene Alvir and the U.P. alumni gave us a luncheon, and we had a book party hosted by the Philippine Embassy. This was held across the old Embassy building on Massachusetts Avenue. Our government had this handsome new office building for a chancery and it was something to be quite proud about.

We could not stay too long with the Dumonts because we had to see our niece Patricia Cruz, in Rockville, Maryland. She is Mrs. Teller now, and she has lived there permanently, raising two children. She is a skillful potter and has had ceramic exhibits. And Pat's husband,

Charles, a consultant for a United Nations department engaged in the development of foods, was preparing for his new assignment in Ethiopia.

One evening, there in Rockville, N.V.M. had a long telephone conversation with Pura Santillan Castrence, for we discovered she was living in nearby Oxon, Maryland. N.V.M. had a piece of sad news to share with her. Our mutual friend S.P. had just died in Manila. It was difficult to tell this to Mrs. Castrence. We did not have the details, to begin with. S.P. had been a life-long friend of hers. All of us went back as far as one afternoon in late November, the afternoon of our tea party at the U.P. Social Hall on Padre Faura. Mrs. Castrence sobbed at the other end of the line, her thoughts and memories going back even much farther.

In New York, N.V.M. gave a reading sponsored by the Academy of American Poets in tandem with the launching of an anthology of Philippine short fiction edited by Luis Francia. Also that evening, Jessica Hagedorn read her selections winning much approval from the audience. Once again, for us, it was an evening of reunions. Morli Dharam, whom we have not seen in years, was a pleasant surprise; he seemed to have thrived in the Big Apple, Bert and Eva Florentino also attended, as did Dr. Harold C. Conklin. The latter came all the way from Princeton with a pair of *kalutang*, the musical sticks of the Mangyans of Mindoro. Harold spent several years of research there, in N.V.M.'s home province. That evening in New York, he and N.V.M. conversed in Tagalog at some length, and in the hearing of quite a number of people, even Asian Society officials, eliciting "ah's" and "oh's", the language being different from what passes for Filipino these days.

The project director of the University of Oregon's International Students Association, Jeffin Arboleda, had arranged for N.V.M. to visit their campus, and to Eugene we proceeded after a few days' rest in Hayward. Racial discrimination, we learned, was stronger in Oregon than in California. Would we find this to be indeed the case?

Would we know, really? We made friends there, though, and among them was Professor Glenn May who supplied us with the information that many valuable items of Filipiniana have been pilfered from the National Library. Over luncheon at the University faculty center, this was a disturbing helping of literary and cultural dish to serve up any visitor. But facts are facts, however it might happen that some are difficult to swallow.

Jeffin arranged a book signing session at the campus store in Oregon, but our biggest evening was in Seattle, at the biggest book store there. It had a reading room, a lecture room and a coffee shop. What a marvelous place to be spending an afternoon browsing, with wonderful coffee within reach. Seattle was a kind of climax for our tour, *The Bread of Salt* having literally seen the light of day there, at the editorial offices of Washington University Press.

Linda Nietes of Philippine Expression, a book store devoted to Filipiniana in Los Angeles, had been with us most days of the tour but we missed her in Seattle and, of course, in Diliman as well, when the time came to launch the U.P. Press edition of the book at U.P.'s Balay Kalinaw. To me, as a writer's wife, this was a time that might be called truly rewarding. Old friends, new friends, faculty members and students—they were all present, demonstrating their affection and loyalty to an aging writer. Billy (Napoleon) Abueva sculpted a flower vase for the occasion that was in the shape of a "G," and at its base the initials "N.V.M."

Narita puts on hood of the Honoris Causa, Doctor for Humane Letters on N.V.M. in 1987

served as an enclosure for a bouquet of fresh flowers. Purita Kalaw Ledesma came all the way from Makati.

U.P. Regent Nelia Gonzalez took time to be present and renew some sort of family ties, no matter how many degrees removed. Old friends and classmates from Araullo High School (in Muralla) came too: Elsa Arellano Syjuco, Dr. Marion Celi de Leon, Maggie Shea, Luchi Fernandez, and Tinay Geslani.

While book launchings and book parties provide satisfaction of a different level to this one writer's wife, there is yet a different kind that comes from children. One day, while searching for material to read to my class of children in the U.P. Literacy Program that Mrs. Emil Javier runs, I found a poem. It was in a workbook entitled *Read, Learn, and Grow - IV*. I copied it and brought it to class. The class was composed of children of varying ages. I started to read the poem "Song," which is a piece by N.V.M. that I had not seen before. Three boys started to recite the poem from memory! I was amazed. "Why do you know this poem?" I asked. Andoy, the boy of the most-likely-to-succeed-type, replied, "Ma'm, I learned it in our Grade V class, in Balara."

On rare get-together nights, at home here in U.P., we celebrate long-standing friendships with music and song. Greg Brillantes and Rene Ira are both wonderful at the piano, and they accompany Nick Joaquin, who has a rich and extensive repertoire of popular music. Lulu Brillantes, Luning Ira, Marra Lanot and I would just hum along. The wonder of it is how Nick Joaquin could remember all the lyrics of those "nineteen forgotten" songs and which we women have not sung in a long, long time.

Although we lived in California for more than twenty years, we have remained Filipino citizens. On one occasion we visited the Philippine Consulate in San Francisco to renew our passports. Eva Betita, who was consul then, observed that we deserved some kind of award for remaining Filipinos after all these years. N.V.M. answered, "I can't be an American citizen if I continue to be a Filipino writer. I am not a Fil-American writer either." His insistence on not being a "hyphenated" writer may have been the reason behind his not being represented in an anthology of Asian American fiction which, later, became a best-seller and went into several editions.

He has more than fulfilled his promise to me, for every child, a book. N.V.M. has other writing projects, his own as well as those of other writers. The final draft for *Iba: The Filipino Short Story in America* has been in the works for some time. N.V.M. felt he could not rush it through as long as he was uncertain about obtaining adequate funds to cover contributor's fees. Only a modest sum is required but it seems difficult to obtain. Authors included in anthologies should be given adequate remuneration, he felt. Without these writers, where would the anthologists be?

N.V.M. at a Philippine Embassy ceremony in Los Angeles, receiving the official copy of a resolution passed by the city council declaring October 11, 1996 as "N.V.M. Gonzalez Day."

N.V.M. seems to be slower now in his "production." After all, he is already past eighty. A few years back, there was not one day when he was not scribbling something or working at his computer. Every day! Sometimes I must appear like a mother hen, checking on his food, both the quality and quantity of it. Or checking his back, as to whether his *camiseta* is wet or not. We spend quite a lot of money for medication. And he also has what he calls "Yamashita's Gold," a brain tumor in his forehead, right beneath the skull. It is benign, and we hope and pray that it remains that way. Please, God! What seems to have worked with us all these years is *shalom bayis*. This is "a Jewish concept of peaceful relationship in the home as an element in the politics of meaning." (Cohen, 1994) I agree heartily with Sara Cohen, author of *Secrets of a Very Good Marriage: Lessons from the Sea*. What really brings that peace is fidelity as practiced by both husband and wife. It's not money, fame, or prestige that count. It is the peace that reigns in the family.

As a writer, what values do N.V.M. live by? He likes to quote his favorite teacher, Sir Herbert Read, the English writer and critic who said, "There's a moral dimension to every English sentence." N.V.M. then adds, "A story or a novel is never finished until it is read. Every story seeks its ideal reader. The reader can often see more in it than is written. His impressions, thoughts and feelings complete the story."

Two years ago at the U.P. Writers Workshop, on Samal Island, we believe we met one such ideal reader. She came all the way from Butuan, Agusan, in order to meet N.V.M. She says she has read all of N.V.M.'s works. Vivian Otaza, left that afternoon to continue teaching English literature. She left a family photograph inscribed: "This is my family, all fully aware of the living legend."

There's another ideal reader, Rosy May Bayuga, N.V.M.'s former student in the Ateneo, who friends call the "Kaingin Girl" because she wrote about the kaingin women in N.V.M.'s fiction for her thesis. Mayette is a good writer herself and has won awards for her stories in Filipino.

So, in marriage, as in his writing, we have values to live by. N.V.M. will continue to write, to teach when asked, to counsel writers who come to him for help. He will continue to write his newspaper columns wherever they are sought for. And he will not stop loving his children and grandchildren and, of course, his other N., "whose greatest contribution in N.V.M.'s art," in the words of Doreen G. Fernandez, "is making it possible for N.V.M. to write."

Julita Quiming Hufana
Marriage Made in Heaven

God has His ways of bringing people together. I believe that God planned from the beginning that Alex and I will be together forever. How else would a skeptic account for my story? Alex had many girl friends, and I had the opportunity of marrying someone else. Yet we were brought together and got married after many years of separation and of being far away from each other. Alex's friends were surprised that no sooner had he arrived in the United States than we were married. Who was this Julita? There were many girls who were running after him, but it was this girl Julita whom he took as his wife.

Alex and Julie Hufana

Alex and I had known each other as early as 1946 when we were in high school. I was fifteen years old when I first met him; he was nineteen. It was at the birthday party of my baby cousin, and Alex came with his friends. My aunt, who was married to his second cousin, rented a room in their house. When my aunt and her family moved out, my uncle and I rented the room they vacated. Their house was near the La Union high school. My uncle was in the fourth year, and I in the second year. Alex was in the third year, just one year ahead of me. His sister and I were in the same year. Although we all went to the same school and were living under one roof like brothers and sisters, Alex never paid me any attention.

On my third year I went to stay at my aunt's house. I hardly saw Alex afterwards and we hardly spoke to each other. I never saw him after he graduated. But I saw him again during the senior prom, and he was busy dancing with other girls. After graduation I stayed for a while at my aunt's house, then returned to my grandfather's and stayed home for a year. I opened a *sari-sari* store. But I wanted to get a job so I left home and went to Manila, where I found work at Mary Johnston Hospital. I met Mrs. Clara Rotz, a dietician; whose husband was a missionary. She invited me to live with them while I took up pre-nursing at the Philippine Christian College. About the time I finished my course, the Rotz family would go back to the United States. They asked me then if I wanted to go to the States. And this I had always wanted, of course. Rev. H. Welton Rotz's parents lived in Hutchinson, Kansas, so it was decided that I would go there. I passed the examination sent to me which I took at the Philippine Christian College. I then enrolled at Grace Hospital School of Nursing in Hutchinson.

Before I left for the United States I visited Alex's mother and sister who were staying in an apartment at Galicia, Sampaloc, Manila. Alex was then in Cebu, teaching in a Chinese school there. His sister insisted that I write to him to say good-bye. Alex was not a stranger to me. His sister was a good friend and treated me like her younger sister. So I wrote Alex.

It was during my second year in Nursing that Alex started writing to me. I was surprised that he wrote at all. I wrote back and that started our letter-writing. After I graduated from nursing school I went to Hastings College in Hastings, Nebraska. We continued to write to each other. He complained that I wrote only facts. He asked for my picture so I sent him a picture of myself leaning against a tree. That probably convinced him that I was no longer the young girl he used to know but was a grown woman now. He sent me a picture; he was still the same person I used to know. He also sent his book of poems, which I shared with my roommate, Helen. I also shared his letters with her.

With a nursing degree, I was assigned by the Presbyterian Board of Foreign Missions to attend several church camps as a foreign representative. The last one I attended was in Cincinnati, Illinois. This was a senior high school camp, and I did some counselling. At the end of the camp I was asked where I wanted to go, so I told them I wanted to go back to New York to meet my boyfriend who was arriving from the Philippines. They thought this was very romantic, and without my knowledge they took a collection. The amount enabled me to go back to New York. I stayed at the women's dorm of Columbia University. My worry was how I would meet Alex at the airport. He wrote that I should meet him there. I didn't even know where Kennedy Airport was. So I went to see Ben Felicitas, who was staying at an apartment hotel. I was looking for his room when I met Maro Santaromana who was looking for a place to stay. I brought him to Ben's room.

The picture that Julie sent Alex, showing a different girl from that kid in La Union.

I learned that Maro was a good friend of Alex and that he would gladly bring me to the airport. Alex's plane was delayed. Alex was with two Filipinos who were staying at the Martinique Hotel. He asked a friend, Remy, if I could stay with her in her room. We talked all night. The next day, we took the bus to the airport to see Alex off. He had been assigned to Elmira, to an American family there, for orientation. I rode with Maro back to Kansas, Illinois, where my foster family lived.

I was set to go to Seattle, where my family was going. But then Alex called and asked me to go to California instead. I decided to go to California where we could know each other better and would decide whether we should really get married. I found a job at Herrick Memorial Hospital in the Obstetrics Department. Alex started school at the University of California in Berkeley, with a scholarship from the Fulbright Foundation. Everything went well. I knew deep in my heart that I loved him and that he loved me. But Alex was spare with those endearing words that a girl in love would like to hear. He might be a poet but he did not recite love poems to me. However, I knew he loved me, so we planned our wedding. We decided to get married on Thanksgiving Day in 1957, which that year fell on November 28. We called Rev. H. Welton Rotz to let him know and he asked whether we could postpone the wedding till December; but this did not appeal to Alex. We found out that Rev. Hessel, who had been a missionary in the Philippines was around. So we approached him and he consented to marry us at the First Presbyterian Church in Berkeley.

Both of us did not have much money; but we went ahead anyway. I did not have money to buy a wedding dress. I wanted white lace so I bought a pattern and the required materials. I sewed my own wedding dress. It was a simple dress but it served the purpose. Our wedding was a very simple affair with about twenty people in attendance. Since there was no entourage but just the two of us, it was decided that we would come out from the two back doors and meet at the altar, with our sponsors. Our promise "to love each other in sickness and in health till death do us part" was before God and witnesses and so there was no turning back for us. Then the pastor said, "What God hath joined together let no man put assunder." That was a seal for life and we had been true to that promise. Alex has always been loyal to his promise.

I thought it was a nice wedding, simple but meaningful for Alex and me. Since it was Thanksgiving Day my uncle cooked turkey; while my sister-in-law and her husband cooked other dishes. We had dinner at my boarding house and that was our wedding reception. Someone bought a wedding cake. After dinner, everyone left. A friend brought us to Pacifica Motel in San Francisco for our honeymoon. I thought Alex spent all his money on my wedding ring but he had enough money for the room. The view was beautiful; it was overlooking the Bay. It was only a weekend honeymoon because Alex had to go back to school and I had to go back to work.

We were both very busy and hardly went out except to buy groceries. There was one occasion as we walked down Shattuck that one evening, I held Alex's hand but he took my hand off and said that "Love is not a public scandal." Alex was never demonstrative, especially in public. In fact, he does not even say endearing words. He calls me by my full name. But that does not mean that he loves me less. Sometimes I ask him if he loves me and his answer is, "Do I, and you still doubt it?" Once in a while I like to hear the words "I love you."

His scholarship ended so we had to go back to the Philippines. Plane tickets were expensive. We took one of the President liners. Alex was seasick, so he stayed in the cabin most of the time. I did not want to stay in the cabin all the time, so I went out to join the games. I could not understand why someone who lived near the sea and swam very well could be seasick on board a big ship. It must be the movement and the smell of the ship because that was how I felt when I got seasick myself.

When we arrived home we stayed with my mother-in-law for a while because there was no vacancy on the U.P. campus. It was difficult for Alex to come home late at night, often after dinner time. He did not have time to look for a place on the campus so I did this myself. Luckily, I found a room in the old Conservatory of Music, in

Area I, where many faculty members lived. It was not a nice place but we had to make do with this room until we could find a better one.

Our first daughter, Aleta, was born while we were living in this place. It was a dark room but we fixed ourselves a living room, a dining room, a kitchen and, most importantly, a bedroom. The bathroom was shared with occupants in the next room. It was quite spooky there, too. We could hear footsteps and the sound of a chain being dragged on the roof. We told our neighbor about all these sounds. One night he went out with his shotgun, but did not hear anything nor see anyone. At first Alex did not believe me so I woke him up in the middle of the night, and he finally believed there was that noise. Alex who came home late in the evening sometimes, and so my cousin and I would go out to the porch to wait for him.

We were glad when finally we moved to one of the rowhouses in Area II. Our two-story apartment was a much better place, indeed except that it was not soundproof. We did not mean to eavesdrop, but we could hear the conversations of our next-door neighbors at night. Probably they too could hear us. They did not complain and we didn't either, so everything went well. There were always some problems, big and small; but we were able to solve them. Alex worked hard, writing up

Alex and Julie in front of one of Alex's paintings

to the wee hours. All the money that he earned he gave to me, getting only his allowance. I took care of everything in the house and also watched our savings. Alex trusted me with everything, and I was thankful for that.

In 1961 Alex was awarded a Rockefeller Foundation Fellowship to do research at the University of California in Berkeley. He did research on Hitler and wrote the book *Sieg Hiel* which was later published. The scholarship was not very much, so I went to work at the Herrick Memorial Hospital. Our second girl, Leni, was born, and due to financial problems I stayed only one day in the hospital after delivery. But I went on vacation for a month. Alex loves his children so he did not mind baby-sitting when I went back to work. He changed the diapers; there were no disposable diapers then. I would make the formula before I left for work so he just warmed the bottles as needed. I worked in the evening on the 3-11 shift, a schedule which worked well with his work. If he needed to go to the library I was home. I cooked dinner before I went to work. He'd put the children to bed. He did not complain about this routine. We tried not to bother Alex when he was writing or reading. Once in a while we went out in our old Chevy. There was a big Safeway nearby, so shopping for groceries was not difficult.

At the end of the year Alex had not finished writing his research so we asked the U.S. Immigration to extend our stay. But this was denied. We even asked Immigration to reverse our status, that I become the provider because I had a job. It was instead recommended that we go on "docket" for six months, and we followed that recommendation. This gave Alex additional time to finish what he was writing. When it was time for us to go back to the Philippines I was pregnant again.

We came home by ship again on board one of the President Lines freighters. We also brought along my mother-in-law, who had been in the States with my sister-in-law. She decided to come home with us. So, on the ship, not only Alex was seasick, but my mother-in-law as well. Imagine me with my big tummy going back and forth to the dining room and to our cabin, carrying food trays for all of us, including my two children. I also had to go wash and dry diapers. I was very glad when we saw land, Kwajalein, one of the Marshall Islands, a U.S. Base. There was nothing to see, except some coconut trees and a store. It was good to get off the ship, especially for those who had been seasick. It was a great feeling to smell fresh air instead of the smell of the ship. This did not last long however, for we had to board the ship to continue our voyage home.

Although we were promised a house, there was no place for us in the U.P. campus when we arrived. We were billeted at the old Women's Dormitory where there were lots of big mosquitoes. In fact, when I reported this to the Quarantine office, they thought I had smallpox! There were new bungalows being built along Apacible St. in Area-3; and as soon as one was finished we moved in. What a relief to get away from the dorm!

When our third daughter, Zayda, was due, Alex was so busy that I had to go to the hospital alone. My friend Conching accompanied me. With three children, Alex's salary was not enough and I had to take in boarders. I rented out one room. When I had enough help, I provided food for our boarders as well as for some of the student boarders who lived at our neighbor's place. Alex was not comfortable with the boarders, but it was what I could think of to help out. It was hard for me to get a regular job with our three children and unstable household help. There were even times when I had to get food from Mila's store on credit, which I paid on payday.

When Alex got a research grant to write I decided to get rid of the boarders and made him a library where he could write, and where his assistant could type in privacy. When he was home he was even busier and spent most of his time in the library. He'd read up to the wee hours. I was now worried about his health. When he was writing, nothing could get him away from what he was doing. He would get mad if I insisted that it was time to go to bed.

Being in the academe, Alex encouraged me to take a master's degree in nursing. I thought this was one way of preventing me from bothering him because I would be busy with my own studies and with the work I had to do until late in the night. I took subjects at the U.P. College of Nursing and finished all the required subjects except thesis writing. I thought I needed to work in order to identify a problem for my thesis, so I taught at the Far Eastern University College of Nursing for two years. But I was so busy preparing for my classes, giving examinations and checking them and correcting term papers that I never got around to do my thesis. On top of that I was pregnant with our fourth daughter, Sharon. I quit my job although I really enjoyed it. During Christmas time my students would come to our house and sing Christmas carols. Alex and the children enjoyed these occasions.

Alex does love to sing. He said that during his younger days, he went serenading with his friends. He has a good voice. When we were renting a room in their house during our high school days, he used to sing as soon as he came home. When we travel, he would sing while driving. Sometimes I would turn off the radio and listen to him sing instead. He likes to sing old songs.

Our income improved when Alex got a part time job, on loan from U.P., as library director of the Cultural Center. He continued to teach at U.P. With these two jobs Alex still found time to write. He also had some books published. When there were presentations at the CCP, and when he could get some free tickets, he'd bring us along. He'd bring us to the library. Sometimes we spent the day with him. We enjoyed these occasions and he liked to show us around. He loves the children and missed them when they were not around. Although he did not talk to them much, he spent quality time with them regularly.

We moved once again to A. Mabini St. where the house was bigger. By this time all the children were in school and I thought of getting a job. I got a teaching job at Capitol Medical Center School of

Nursing. I was also a Coordinator between the school and the hospital. One of the faculty members suggested to the principal to abolish the position of coordinator. And so it was that the position was abolished. I felt that the students did not have enough follow-up in the hospital. I resigned from my teaching post.

As a library director, Alex needed to have a degree in Library Science so his boss got him a Rockefeller Scholarship, a third scholarship for his master's degree in Library Science at Columbia University in New York. The children and I went along with him. The scholarship allowance was not enough for all of us, so I got my New York R.N. registration and worked. We were allowed to bring along a maid with us to help me take care of the children. I was not supposed to work but I had to because the money was never enough. Rent in Manhattan was high and so we moved to Queens at Staten Island. Alex and I had to take the ferry every day to go to Manhattan, for him to go to school, and for me to go to work. Then we took the subway to our respective destinations. We liked Staten Island, the air was fresher and the weather was not very cold. Our three children went to school there, except Sharon who was too young and stayed home with the maid.

When Alex graduated, the Rockefeller scholarship arranged an itinerary for him to visit Cultural Libraries in the East and in the West. This brought us to California. We went to Los Angeles, and to save some money, we stayed in my father's house for three months. Then we went to Oakland where we were able to rent a room from a Filipino couple. The children continued with their schooling during all the moves we made. I was able to work again. At one time when I was not working, Alex brought me with him to Monterey where we met a very nice American couple at whose house we stayed.

After his scholarship it was time to go home. I wanted to stay longer in the US, but Alex being nationalistic and loyal to his word would not hear of it. Once he set his mind on going home, it was futile to change it.

When we came home I did not have a job, so I took the opportunity of using the privilege of my being the wife of a faculty member and went back to school. This time I pursued a course in Social Work, a diploma course in Community Development. Whatever I planned, Alex approved. He did not say anything against it. Alex was very glad when I received my diploma and I was also proud that I finished a course in U.P., where all our children were enrolled.

Aside from writing, Alex enjoys painting. When he gets tired of painting he goes to writing and vice versa. I was happy to buy him painting materials. He sold some paintings to his friends. He also had exhibits. When Eva Florentino invited me to join her in a gallery at the Asian Institute of Tourism, Alex was happy. Although I knew nothing about art, Eva assured me that it was all right because she was with me.

When we first came back from the States, we bought a piece of residential lot in Tandang Sora. We decided it was time that we build our own house. Alex borrowed some money from Pag-Ibig Fund and some from a bank. But Pag-Ibig wanted us to start the construction before they would release the loan. We had to borrow money from other sources in order to get the Pag-Ibig loan. So we had to sell our land in Taytay to add to the amount to start the construction of the house. Alex left everything to me and, in order to save, I bought the materials myself and supervised the workers. I reported to him what was going on; he came to see the work once and was satisfied with what he saw. He trusted me in supervising the building of our home. I had to tell him what was being done and sometimes his suggestions came very late.

Before the house was finished our oldest daughter Aleta got married to Duffie Osental. Alex could hardly give his consent because she had just finished college. But she was of age. We were sad about it, but there was nothing we could do except give her our blessings. She had a big wedding and everyone was happy. But when we went home I felt so empty, knowing that she will not come home to us again. Alex was very quiet and sad but we consoled each other and thought that we still had three daughters who were still with us.

Alex was always busy even when he was home. He was always in the CCP library. When he was not at home, he was in meetings with his writer friends. He usually got drunk. Sometimes he invited me to these meetings, but his friends smoked so much they filled the room with cigarette smoke. When he went by himself he'd come home very drunk. He'd vomit all over the floor or in the bathroom. I had to clean up.

On special occasions like birthdays and anniversaries, Alex brought us out to eat. He enjoyed eating out, too. I am not a very good cook, so going out to eat was a respite from my cooking. Sometimes I also got tired of my own cooking. Besides, going out made life more enjoyable and less boring. Alex often forgot birthdays and anniversaries and I always had to remind him about this.

We had some problems finishing our house in Tandang Sora because we did not know where to get additional funds. The Lord is good to us; when Alex had an exhibit, the biggest painting on display, the *Two Fighting Horses*, was bought by his boss. The amount helped us finish the house and we were glad to move in. Alex was happy for there was more space for him to move around the house and in the garden. We had a high wall and the neighbors could not see us. Alex is not a very sociable individual. He is only sociable with his friends and colleagues; he is happy when he is with them.

Alex retired from the U.P. and the Cultural Center at the age of sixty. After fifteen years of waiting we were told by the United States Embassy that we could now immigrate to the United States, based on the application filed by his sister. Even if Alex could not work in the U.S., I still could. We brought along our youngest daughter, who was eighteen years old. Our other daughter was over twenty-one years old, so she was not permitted to join us. We went to Los Angeles where our daughter went to school to finish her college education. Luckily she was able to get a scholarship. I found a job as registered nurse. It was difficult for Alex to get a job and we thought it was because of his age. The Americans are prejudiced, even if they say that they are not, about old age.

He was at times frustrated when he couldn't get a job. I did not mind if he did not work because he was always busy writing. I was getting enough for our subsistence. I consoled him by telling him that he had his retirement pension from U.P. anyway and not to worry about money. He finally got a job at a vocational college and taught English. Then there was another job for him where I was working, as a medical records employee. He was happy that he was able to contribute financially to the family income.

Alex came home to the Philippines when he gave away, our second daughter Leni, to Patrick del Prado in marriage. When he came back he reported to me that it was a nice wedding. Then our third daughter, Zayda, got married too without our presence, not because we did not want to come home but because she and Dennis Abenoja got married by themselves without their families around. They did not even tell her grandmother where they were staying at that time. We accepted her decision since we realized that young people now just do what they want to do.

We left someone to take care of our house in Tandang Sora, but we learned that it was not well cared for. We decided to sell the house and get rid of this problem.

With the money we were able to make a downpayment for our house in Long Beach, California. Alex was out of work again, so he did the cooking for us. When I arrived home from work, the food was ready. He was proud of his cooking. I had to show my appreciation, for fear he might say "You do it" yourself. He sang while he was cooking as if he was really enjoying it. He cooked well and wanted us to eat what he prepared.

Alex enjoyed driving and going places. When our daughter Aleta and her family were in Palm Springs, we used to drive there whenever it was my day off. It was a respite from an otherwise boring existence. Even when Alex was busy with his writing, he felt the boredom of just staying at home. Staying home gave me time to rest, for I went to work five days a week. Sometimes we drove to the mall where we either shopped or just went window-shopping. We hardly went to the movies. We watched favorite T.V. programs at night. Alex enjoys boxing and would not miss watching those championship fights. Although I wanted to watch something else the fights were a priority.

At Sharon's wedding: Alex, his mother, Julie and the girls

Alex and I share a love for travel. Alex wanted to see New York again and so did I. So off we went and saw some old friends. Our relatives brought us to Atlantic City and New Jersey, then we went around New York City. We went to Columbia University, Alex's Alma Mater, and were really glad to see it once again. He showed me around and was very proud of it. We also rode the ferry and reminisced the times when we were daily passengers. We went around Staten Island and found a new shopping mall. We could have gone around longer, but Alex had a gout attack and could not walk. So he stayed home while I went out with my relatives.

Before going back to California, we took a train to South Carolina to pick up my uncle to help him drive his car. He did not tell us that his car was an old one but we drove it anyway. The car gave us so much trouble all the way. It took us a week to reach California. Then we ran out of cash! California checks could not be cashed outside of California. We were glad when we finally reached California and had the car towed to our destination. Alex was very mad, but there was nothing we could do. It was an experience that we did not want repeated.

At another time we drove to Northern California and stopped in Chico to see his uncle and his family. He is married to an Indian-German-American. They were all glad to see each other. Alex also saw his two cousins and we all had a good time. Alex's uncle who is his mother's only brother had never been back to the Philippines since he left. He is now in his 80's. Then we went on to Pittsburgh, California, where my aunt and her husband live. It was so hot that they brought us to San Francisco to cool off. They also brought us to Yosemite, where it was much cooler. When we went back to Pittsburgh, Alex felt so hot that we thought he would have an attack. So it was time for us to go back to Carson. Although Alex did not mind driving back, I was very worried because it would have been very difficult for him if he had an asthma attack.

When Alex was sixty-five years old, he started having health problems. One time he could not breathe and we had to call 911. He was brought to the hospital and had an intubation before he was brought to the Intensive Care Unit. A respirator helped him overcome his difficulty in breathing. The doctor said he has chronic obstructive pulmonary disease (COPD), emphysema and asthma. Besides his asthma, which he acquired at an early age, his other illnesses were due to his smoking. These illnesses were irreversible and he suffered from them all through life.

When our youngest daughter Sharon got married to Rolando Espejo, Jr., we decided to sell our Long Beach house. Unluckily, there was a slump in the real estate business. We would not get much from the sale, not even from equity. So we applied for foreclosure, packed all our things and sent them to the Philippines. We stayed at Sharon and Jun's house temporarily until she gave birth to her son, our eighth grandchild. We enjoyed taking care of our new grandson. We came back to the Philippines when he was 11 months old.

This was in August, and it was hot and humid. Alex got very sick, so he was brought to the Lung Center. He could not breathe; again he was intubated and attached to a respirator at the ICU. He was very much weakened and had to rest before he could travel again. We were supposed to go to San Fernando, La Union, our destination. La Union is not as polluted as Metro Manila, so we thought he would be better to live there. The doctor told us that we had come home in the wrong month because it was asthma season.

Alex kept getting sick now even in the province. We went in and out of the hospital. I resorted to having a doctor come to the house, to start an I.V. injection. This way I could just take care of him at home. His poor health worried me a lot and made my already high blood pressure worse. At home, Alex had an oxygen tank and a nebulizer, plus all medications prescribed by his doctor. Our room was better than the hospital with its air-conditioning, however.

When Alex was stronger and somewhat recovered, we decided to go back to the States so he could recuperate. We stayed home most of the time. Our daughter and our grandson visited occasionally. They bought us out to dinner or to go shopping. We bought a car which gave us freedom of movement. We visited our daughter and her family on weekends in Garden Grove. At first I would drive but Alex would take over the driving when he was stronger and felt that he could do it without having shortness of breath. Thank God he did not get sick except once, when we were almost back home from one of our visits. He felt sick because he caught a cold. The doctor advised him to seek admission in the hospital for I.V. medications. He stayed in the hospital for one week.

Once in a while when he was feeling better we went out to eat hamburger. As senior citizens we enjoyed a good discount. Alex loves fruits, so we'd go to a grocery that sold cheap fruits. We had fruits all the time. We miss the fruits now that we are back in the Philippines. Sometimes we went to the movies. One advantage about being in the States is our lifetime health insurance, but it is functional only when we are in the States. We cannot avail ourselves of medicare privilege outside the United States. We applied for a private insurance that could cover us for at least three months outside the States. Medicare does not cover prescriptions which the private insurance does. Alex needs medications which cost quite a lot of money. The private insurance covers the oxygen that Alex now needs every night.

Alex has accepted that now he is an invalid of some sort, who needs to have his oxygen every night. When it is hot he needs air-conditioning in the room. He must not miss his medications. He could not walk far because he tires easily and has difficulty breathing. But he keeps busy all the time, always trying to meet deadlines.

I have accepted Alex, with all his angst, (he's a poet I know), his strong likes and dislikes, and his bad moods and words, which hurts especially when I am tired and stressed out.

Today, we accept our being old. Only God knows when our time on earth will end, and we return to our Maker. Till then we have to continue with what we are doing, and hope that all these please our Maker.

Edna May Obien-Landicho
Music to my Ears

❧☙

It was one hot summer of 1968. I was then only 21. Through the proddings of my mother and sister who were also teachers like myself, I enrolled for my masters degree at the National Teachers College in Manila. It was then that I met my husband. He was teaching in the same college and also taking his M.A. We became classmates in Advanced Educational Psychology.

In no time at all he started courting me. But I was in no mood for any romantic involvement as yet. But he persisted and before the summer term ended I had known him a little bit more—an aspiring fictionist. He even showed me a copy of a magazine where one of his works was published.

I left Manila with mixed feelings for him.

In December of the same year, he surprised us when he came to my hometown in Sigma, Capiz. There is no lodging place in the town and he became our house guest. I thought it was just a visit, a Christmas vacation. But I was wrong.

Domingo and Edna May Landicho

Edna May, her mother, Doming and their children and grandchildren

Before he left for Manila, he proposed marriage to me, a civil marriage. I did not know what got into me but I accepted his proposal and I told my parents about it. Naturally, they strongly objected. They were so concerned that the town would misconstrue the whole thing and that I was still very young although I was already on my third year of teaching in the public schools. Deep down I knew, my parents were not ready to lose me to someone, a virtual stranger to them, who lives miles away. I also knew that they secretly wished that I end up with a local boy, the former boyfriend who was again trying to make a comeback.

Since my parents would not budge a bit from their decision, we decided to go on with the idea anyway with the help of some friends who were also teachers. We got married in a neighboring town, with the municipal judge who officiated our marriage as our principal sponsor.

April the following year, we had our church wedding. We were married in the Bishop's Palace in Roxas City, with the then Bishop officiating the wedding. The following day, I flew to Manila with my husband—a man whom I hardly knew and whom I will share life and fate with.

It was a hard, trying start of a married life. Teaching on a meager salary, my husband tried hard to augment his income by writing. I started teaching in an elementary school in Tondo. In the evenings, I continued my masteral study. He did the same. Then we would go home to our first abode, an apartment in Pananalig Street, a place between Sta. Ana and Mandaluyong which easily got flooded during rainy days.

It was there where I got a taste of hard life. Both of us continued supporting our younger siblings—mine in Panay, his in Batangas and Manila. The apartment was so bare—no refrigerator, only cheap furniture and a one-burner electric stove. Our bed was an old, rickety steel bed, with very thin matting.

My husband had a very small typewriter. It was without a handle for spacing so he would manually roll the two sides of the typing machine for correct spacing. On top of this difficulty, he would use the bed as his typing table since we did not have a table for this purpose. Because the steel bed is for a single person, I had to lie on my side while he was typing. The room was so small for us because the two bigger rooms were occupied by his relatives, who were either studying or working or both, in Manila.

Before the start of the big rains, we left Pananalig Street and transferred to the house of my aunt who left for the U.S. The house was also in Mandaluyong, a few blocks away from Edsa.

It was a comfortable bungalow in a corner of a 700-square-meter lot with fruit-bearing trees around. When we got there, we built a small *sari-sari* store. Because there was enough space, my husband also started a small piggery.

During this time, I became pregnant. And there was an interesting development in the life of my husband. He became involved in the labor movement in his school. He became an officer of the faculty labor union. Soon, they held a strike when there was a gridlock in the negotiation with the management. I remembered bringing food to the picket line for my husband and his fellow picketeers. It was really a very strange twist of fate for me. I was to deliver a baby by June and my husband was in the thick of a labor struggle. But I had to be strong under the circumstances. I am his wife and I have learned to stand up with him—no matter how strange it was to me at the start.

I knew that they won the economic demands of the faculty union because there was a small raise in their hourly pay.

But the shocking development in our life was soon to unfold. That summer of 1970, my husband was not given any teaching load. He would not earn a single centavo for summer. And there I was, about to give birth in June.

It was really a test of strength, patience, character and faith. My husband became an insurance underwriter for a prestigious company. He also ventured into "life-plan" underwriting which was then quite a new idea. He was overjoyed when he said that Satur Ocampo bought an insurance policy of P100,000, and Butch del Castillo and Henry Romero got theirs too. My husband told me that those friends of his bought policies to help him, nothing more. (It was only now that I know what my husband meant when he told me those things.)

The Landichos and children

During the next schoolyear, my husband became a lecturer at the Philippine College of Commerce (now Polytechnic University of the Philippines), and the University of the Philippines in Diliman. And came a new threshold of our journey as a young family.

This time, my husband became involved in the activist movement. He would recite poems at demonstrations. There were times when he would come home haggard-looking and smelled of teargas. There were nights when he would not come home at all. He would later tell me that he had been invited to talk at some special gatherings.

I also got involved in a way in what he was doing. When I was pregnant with our second child, I would walk from the Rotunda in Quezon City to Agrifina Circle in Luneta in mass actions. I joined demonstrations simply because I wanted to know the strange world and beliefs of my husband.

When the writ of habeas corpus was suspended, I was so thankful that my husband was not incarcerated. So many people wondered why he was spared, as his being the founding chairman of the Panulat Para sa Kaunlaran ng Sambayanan (PAKSA) was so known, and his participation in mass actions was so public and visible.

But one evening he came back. I thought that, like before, he would soon leave again. But my husband stayed.

Then he pounced on his typewriter once more. He became an active writer again. He went back to teaching at the same time.

I remember that day when I gave birth to our second child, in a clinic in Mandaluyong. The day before, there was a big rally held in Plaza Miranda. My husband was supposed to recite a poem in that rally. But he stayed with me in the hospital—until our daughter was born.

On September 21, 1972 Martial Law was declared. I remember how alarmed we were when we saw on a television news program that one of the books banned by the martial law administration was my husband's first published book, a slim volume of winning short stories, *Himagsik*. We would later discover that it was not even allowed to be read inside the library of the State University.

But this time, my husband seemed to be single-minded in his purpose in life: to teach and to write. When the University opened its gates again, he went back to teaching. And he continued his writings.

It was during this period when my husband branched out to other literary genres. He started writing articles for publications. Soon he was writing a regular column in a Tagalog newspaper.

It was also during this period when he encouraged me to write. And I did. I used my maiden name. As a native Visayan, I was a bit unsure of my Tagalog—but he urged me to go on until I felt comfortable with the language.

During this period of our married life, my own artistic interests in a way played a role in my husband's career as a dramatist and as an actor too.

I was really interested in theater. From writing and directing plays in my school in Tondo, I became the educational media curriculum scriptwriter for the Division of City Schools in Manila. This responsibility necessitated broad knowledge of theater, as well as the other arts. So I got involved in theater through the Philippine Educational Theater Association (PETA).

My husband only accompanied me at the beginning. But soon, he was enticed to get involved himself in theater. He got his first taste of theater experience in Amelia Bonifacio's play on Andres Bonifacio which was directed by Behn Cervantes. Then he became a member of the PETA too, as one of its in-house playwrights. But being in the organization, he must be all-around in his involvement. Like everyone else, he became involved in various

The Landicho family in 1996

aspects of theater—and during this short period of time, from 1976 to 1978, he was able to write three full-length plays on Andres Bonifacio, one *sarsuela*, *Sumpang Mahal*, which was produced by the U.P. Concert Chorus, *Dupluhang Bayan*, produced by PETA and *Toreng Garing*, produced by Dulaang U.P.

Both of us have been so engrossed with our involvement in theater that we considered Raha Sulayman Theater in Fort Bonifacio our second home—every night, rain or storm. Until one day, we both realized that the children, four of them this time, needed our attention at home.

It was my husband who decided that we stopped our involvement in the theater world. We both stopped our theater passion suddenly and absolutely —and stayed with the children.

My husband stopped writing plays. But because of my interest in children's culture, I continued writing plays for children, first as a writer of *Kulit Bulilit*, an educational television show for children and then as a teacher of theater at U.P.

This time my husband became obsessed in finishing his first major novel, which he had started writing almost two decades ago. He enrolled in a Ph.D. program in Philippine Studies with a very unique idea in mind. He would like to write his dissertation in the form of a novel.

When he first submitted *Anak ng Lupa* as a dissertation proposal sometime in the early '70s, it was not accepted. He stopped writing the novel—and stopped dreaming to pursue his Ph.D. studies.

But after 18 years he resumed his doctoral studies. I felt he took it up again because I was myself enrolled in my own Ph.D. program. He certainly did not like to be left behind. He again submitted the old proposal and this time it was accepted.

He was able to graduate, and with a novel about his own barrio, his own birth place, to boot.

Looking back, it has been really a very wonderful experience being married to a writer. Certainly, we have our ups and downs—but we always manage to forge ahead.

My husband has a way of charting our lives. He always involves me in so many things. He encourages me to be a writer, too, perhaps because he likes me to understand him better.

But to my mind, my husband has a very normal lifestyle, even at the thick of his writing activity.

Of course, he is no longer using our bed as a typing table. But he works right inside our room—in a small corner truly his own.

We have two computers in our room, but he would not touch them. He would still cling to his old manual typewriter (though not the same one that we started with), and in my sleep, I could still hear its small noises, which after 30 years I already had become accustomed to and could be considered some kind of music to my ears.

He has no fixed hours for writing. Every little minute is a minute of writing for him. And every minute, he can be disturbed—especially by his children when they ask him to do something.

It has always been that way. He would sit before his typewriter, and his children, especially our second child, May, would ask him to do a favor for her. He would oblige without a trace of chagrin. May is now 28 years old and already working, but she still asks her Dad to shine her shoes while her Dad is in front of his old typewriter. And now it's not only his children who can yank him from his typewriter but also his four grandchildren—six-year old twin boys Dyno and Delyno, nine-month old Ian and one-year old Bea. The lovable tykes would take turns slipping into his lap and pound on the keys while he is in the midst of a very important literary creation or scholarly work.

And yes, after all those long, long years, my husband is still urging me to write—a novel about my barrio in Sigma, Capiz, and after finishing this feature article, a biography about him.

And to me, it is a wonderful idea, writing about a lifetime partner who has done a lot to make me blossom into what I am now.

Alma Cruz Miclat
Peking Apple

Alma and Mario in New York, 1996

I was sitting on a sofa looking at the nurse rubbing his soles with gauze soaked in alcohol and water. He was running a 42°C fever and was muttering gibberish. A bottle of dextrose hung on the left side of the bed in the private room reeking with Lysol. I was heavy with my first baby and was just out of the hospital after a threatened miscarriage.

I stood up, looked at the window, and saw the darkness of a Beijing winter night. The Sanlingyao Yiyuan, Hospital No. 301, a military hospital catering to the People's Liberation Army cadres and foreign "comrades," was located in a forlorn suburb west of Beijing in the direction of Babaoshan, the Mountain of Eight Treasures Cemetery. I could discern the outline of the big poplars, leafless and winterdead. The black stillness of the night broken by the occasional hooting of straggling blackbirds heightened my desolation. I felt a lump in my throat. I finally let out a muffled cry, careful not to disturb the silence of the night. Twenty-five years of my life shared with my husband, Mario, has always been a roller-coaster of feelings, the lows usually happening during his own lows. I feared that Mario's first hospitalization during our first winter in the Chinese capital in 1971 would be his last. Images of a very young woman bringing up her baby all by herself, kept me awake the whole night of my vigil by his sickbed.

He was all *joie de vivre* earlier in the day, excited at the first appearance of the sun in all its glorious warmth, or so it seemed from the glass panelled windows of our room at the Foreign Experts' Building where we usually rest after lunch. The long days of leaden sky were over! Piece by heavy piece, he took off his thick padded clothes until only his long johns remained. He deliciously basked in the sun. He and I would never forget that bitter lesson. Yes, the sun shone even in winter, the outside temperature remained sub-zero even at noon, and scanty clothing spelled *ganmao,* the Peking flu.

Mario would survive his first *ganmao,* but would be vulnerable to the bitter cold, or to sudden changes in temperature even after coming back home to the Philippines after our fifteen long years of exile in China.

I MET Mario in one of the teach-ins at the University of the Philippines during the height of the First Quarter Storm. His eloquence and good looks preceded him. I thought I knew him from what I was overhearing from my dorm mates at the Kamia Residence Hall in the Diliman campus. A young poet and writer, former councillor of the College of Arts and Sciences and the founding editor of the college paper, *Sinag,* he was the "crush *ng bayan."*

I was just then starting to digest the political jargon being spewed out everywhere in the liberal atmosphere of the university. Having just joined the Progresibong Samahan sa Inhinyeriya at Agham (PSIA), I was active at discussions and attentive to speakers, mostly from the Student Cultural Association of the University of the Philippines (SCAUP) where Mario was a stalwart. He was indeed an eloquent speaker and storyteller. As presented by him, the history of our country which I felt was a boring topic before, came to life. He told us anecdotes on the Philippine revolution and the Filipino heroes as though he had been present in all the incidents he was relating. He had an eye for detail, touching my heartstrings, which never happened before in the history classes I took at the State University.

I craved for more learning. I listened to other fiery speakers—Monico Atienza, Lito Alvarez, Fluellen Ortigas, Nonie Villanueva and others. The core organization which handled the lectures might have noticed my naive enthusiasm because I was later included in an evening discussion group (DG) with my cousin, Rolly, and friend Tanggol. Mario was assigned as our DG leader, presenting and explaining in a most logical, if "brainwashing" way, leftist phrases and lingo which sounded intimidating, like "Marxism-Leninism," "dialectical materialism," "law of surplus value," "bourgeoisie vs. proletariat." I felt that a whole new world was opened to me. I got hooked.

I also began to be interested in what Mario was writing. I read his poems and short stories, both in English and Filipino, published in the campus newspaper, *Collegian*. His *"Dahil sa 'La Oro' sa North Diversion Road"* was so different from the usual short stories. His views on many aspects of life were new to me, widening my cultural horizon. We watched movies like *Cromwell, Battle of Algiers* and *Burn*. He would then engage me in long discussions about the merits and demerits of those historical films in relation to, let's say, the methods of Soviet actor, director and producer, Konstantin Stanislavsky.

Soon, Mario would take me to the printing presses, one of which was Ka Amado Hernandez's newspaper, *Ang Masa*, where he served as managing editor. A cubbyhole tucked away in an unassuming side street of Sta. Mesa was printing *Mga Siniping Pangungusap ng Tagapangulong Mao,* the *Little Red Book,* where we would go deep in the night for him to proofread. I must say that those forays would transpire only after he had courted me and I had answered affirmatively. I believed he only wanted to be politically correct.

He was always busy those First Quarter Storm days, always out of town for days on end. But he would be sending me notes through common friends. He often came up with poems, busy as

Mario and Alma in Beijing, winter 1973

he was. One poem, *"Pagbabalikwas"* would be put into music and sung like an anthem in street plays, demonstrations and other gatherings, even as we have left for China to venture into another life.

The ancient Minerva printing machine used in the very first Filipino version of *Little Red Book* would be similar to the antiquity used by the Foreign Languages Press in Beijing when Mario retranslated it based on the Chinese text with the help of some Chinese colleagues from Radio Peking.

OUR FIRST year in China was a period of great expectations and big adjustments not only in climate, political and otherwise, food, and way of life but also in our personal relationship. Mario and I went to China as a young married couple, having just wedded in a most unconventional way three months before.

We spent our first two months in the People's Republic touring Beijing and the suburbs and attending our first National Day celebrations at Tiananmen Square. On October 26, 1971, we started working in the Philippine Section of Radio Peking as *waiguo chuanjia*. This Chinese term translates into "foreign expert" and was liberally used for foreigners working not only in the Ministry of Radio, Film and Television which housed Radio Peking but in all units. The terminology should be more appropriately termed as "jack of all trades" for in the succeeding years we would see ourselves as adviser on Philippine affairs, translator, feature writer, editor, copyreader, broadcaster, Filipino grammar and voice teacher, recording technician, all rolled into one. Mario would be at his best doing all these as he had experience preparing and broadcasting the radio program of the Movement for a Democratic Philippines at DZME before we left for China. Meanwhile, greenhorn me would trail like his shadow. The section comprised of seven overseas Chinese from the Philippines who have returned "to the embrace of their motherland" in the '60s, and five native Chinese, who graduated from the Radio Peking Institute with Tagalog as their major and Russian as their minor language.

Our routine work in the Radio was a most welcome change in what was becoming a humdrum existence in a big house provided to us by the Chinese in a most exclusive tightly guarded compound in western Beijing. The compound named *Shibasuo* (Eighteen Villas) was huge yet nondescript when viewed from outside. It was a haven of trees—poplars, pines, apples, walnuts and persimmons—in number inversely proportional to that of the residents of the compound. Only four out of the eighteen villas were occupied at that time we arrived in Beijing. The villa was a two-storey affair with a big receiving room, a TV and radio room, conference room, spacious library, pantry, large kitchen with an enormous oven, a big dining room, and bedrooms with bathrooms as big as two table tennis courts.

I was having prenatal blues and was losing weight. Every time I partook of the greasy dishes of the northern China cuisine, I threw up. To think that we were supposed to have the best cooks in the land. One time, while Mario and I were taking a walk inside the compound, I took a fancy to the unripe little green apples hanging

The Miclat family at the Foreign Experts Compound, Beijing, late autumn 1979

temptingly from the trees around the compound. Mario picked some for me and I ate and enjoyed the fruit for the first time since we arrived in Beijing. In no time, one of the attendants taking care of us in our house brought a basketful of big, luscious red apples. He warned us not to touch the apples in the trees for they were sprayed with DDT. It turned out that the People's Liberation Army men (PLA) guarding Shibasuo had seen Mario pick the little apples. They were to be distributed to the residents when the fruits eventually ripen. I did not eat the red apples as they were too sweet for comfort and my heart cried out for the unripe sour ones. In fact, it was green mangoes I was longing for.

WE ARRIVED in China midway through the turbulent Great Proletarian Cultural Revolution—GPCR or Cultural Revolution, for short. During our first celebration of China's National Day on October 1, we were very excited when told by our interpreter that Chairman Mao, "the Great Helmsman," always appeared at the balcony of Tiananmen Square, side by side with his closest comrade-in-arms and successor, Lin Piao, during such celebrations.

The absence of China's two paramount leaders, during the subdued National Day celebration, became a subject of much speculation by China watchers. We would hear later from the *Voice of America* and the BBC conjectures that Mao was very sick, and that Lin Piao had died in an airplane crash at Ulan Bator, Mongolia while fleeing after a coup against Mao earlier in September. Our own Radio Peking would have no single word about this until many months later.

We witnessed the consolidation phase of the Cultural Revolution as led by the ultra-leftist group in the Chinese Communist Party, later to be known as the "Gang of Four." The first entertainment fare we had was an acrobatics show, which was also the first to be shown after such shows were banned in the first five years of the revolution. The jugglers would miss their jars, and the tight-rope walkers would repeatedly go back to the starting platform before they could finish their routine. And such mistakes were not just play-acting. Later on, we would be asked to grace the opening of the acrobatics stunts from all the provinces which could possibly mount similar shows. Of course, the Shenyang, Beijing and Chungking acrobats would later develop into world class troupers.

And then there were four revolutionary Peking operas. The first that we saw was *Shachiapang* followed by *The Red Lantern*. Both were novelties for us. We welcomed them at the beginning with enthusiasm, together with two full-length "revolutionary" ballets, the "Red Detachment of Women" and "White-Haired Girl," plus a "revolutionary" symphonic suite, "Ode to the Yellow River."

The novelty, however, would wear off after we were treated with the same cultural fare in all the invitations we would receive. The best group from this province or that would be performing the model operas at this exclusive theater or that. The only television station available then which was broadcasting a few days a week for a few hours in the evening would also feature the same four operas and two ballets and a sprinkling of documentaries on the war against Japan and on liberation.

The cultural revolution turned out to be a cultural desert for a vast country of one fourth of humanity. As foreign "comrades," we would be regularly treated to weekly exclusive showing of films from Albania, and later, also from Vietnam, North Korea and Romania, the only remaining allies of China offering more or less "politically correct" cultural fares. But even these were not easily made available to ordinary Chinese.

We were not ready for the stifling atmosphere in what we thought would be the bastion of a liberating socialism and world revolution. Our attempts to engage our Radio colleagues in discussions on China's state of affairs were stonewalled. We tried to discuss with them, for example, the revolutionary exploits of the "Great Helmsman's successor" and felt like speaking Greek (or Szechuanese for that matter). We could sense agitation in their nervous laughter when we paid them unexpected visits at their homes. Only much later would we learn from them that they would be visited by the party commissar or the militia for interrogation after such visits.

There was also aggravation on the use of the language in the broadcast beamed to the Philippines. Mario would forever debate with them on the nuances of Filipino words and grammatical construction. While the ones who came from the Philippines and were very fluent in Filipino would surreptitiously nod in agreement, the head of the Section, a

Mario and Alma, with the Great Wall in the background, spring 1982

Communist Party member of peasant descent, and one of the peasant graduates from Radio Peking Institute, would say that he had to get approval first from the higher-ups on the subject, people who did not know the language in the first place.

Of course, we would be hearing a lot of stories of violent excesses of the ultra-leftists and the campaign against the "four olds" (old culture, old ideas, old customs, and old habits) spawned by the GPCR. But the story which would affect me in so many ways was very close to home.

YUAN WAS a Chinese colleague in the Radio who was an enigma to us. In her forties, we learned that she used to be a vocal music teacher when she was still living in the Philippines. She had had voice training by the great Jovita Fuentes herself. She was one of the seven overseas Chinese in the Philippine Section of the Radio Peking who, out of patriotic fervor, left the Philippines and returned to their motherland to help in the socialist construction. Like all other women in China during those days, she wore fatigue green or blue baggy pants and jackets. But somehow she carried hers with aplomb.

Yuan was very solicitous, always asking about my health, my needs as an infanticipating young girl. She would talk to us about the Philippines, about her work, about her voice teachers, her intense love for music, and about so many things under the sun. These talks helped ward off our homesickness. I warmed up to her immediately. What was strange was that nobody seemed to want to talk to her except us. She was virtually a pariah.

In the Radio, our routine was to prepare and translate into Filipino the Chinese news, commentaries and features from the Hsinhua News Agency. That was all usually done in the office in the morning. Afternoon was for voice recording in the studio, and picking out the pre-selected pieces of music as time-filler. Yuan had a beautiful voice and I would often ask her to join us in coaching the announcers or to do the reading herself. She would forever make up excuses so as not to be with us in the recording studio. Later, we would learn that she was banned from entering the studio.

It turned out that Yuan had been the former head of the Philippine Section. When the Cultural Revolution started in 1966, she was forced by the Red Guards to wear a dunce cap and paraded around the Radio compound with head bowed and with Chinese script in front and at the back of her body declaring her "political crime." She was accused of cultural decadence for possessing a "Western voice" because of her background in European and Philippine classical music. All this we would learn only later, as she never breathed a word to us of her political persecution.

In spite of limitations imposed on Yuan, we managed to get close to her and to visit her house which was bigger than the one-room apartment of most Chinese but still smaller than the size of two table tennis courts. Always fascinated by her voice and intrigued by what she could sing, I prodded her to sing for us. She obliged by singing "La Vie En Rose", but not before sealing with a quilt their bedroom, which also served as their receiving room, to muffle any sound that would emanate from it. She had an ethereal voice that sent me soaring up the sky. She then asked her elder boy to play the violin. I was transfixed by the music of Paganini, the rhythm reverberating in my mind long after her whole family was allowed to leave China for Hongkong after the Cultural Revolution. In my visit to Hongkong years later, the boy, already a grown man, would haunt me once again with his music. He was now a first violinist of the Hongkong Philharmonic Orchestra.

Mario did not want me to record such anecdotes in my small diary. He was afraid that if found by others, the diary would be misconstrued as notes of a spy, or a class enemy, or a counter-revolutionary. In the same ghetto where the Yuans lived, a Radio cadre was persecuted as a "counter-revolutionary enemy" because of a little remark told during their family dinner. He said the big wart on Chairman Mao's chin might be cancerous. The remark, repeated by the hapless man's son to his kindergarten classmates was overheard by their teacher who in turn relayed it to the authorities. The comment was interpreted as a secret longing for the Chairman's death. Inadvertently or otherwise, neighbors spied on neighbors, family members, on one another, to advance the "dictatorship of the proletariat."

I would not know when Mario would start taking down notes himself about the human miseries brought about by the cultural revolution, notes that would be fodder for some of his stories later on. He eventually brought home such notes, taken during his long stint in the countryside about some harrowing experiences.

Our eldest daughter, Maningning was five when Mario came home from more than a year's stay in a state farm. Earlier, Mario suggested that we go stay in a commune for some time to have a taste of peasant life and the revolution in the countryside. Ningning and I went with him to Hunan for a month and went back to Beijing, leaving him in a state farm. A year after, thinner and much older, Ningning couldn't recognize him; she preferred his picture, which she kept by her bedside table. He was diagnosed as suffering from primary complex. I had to learn to give injections and administer the streptomycin shots he needed twice a day. Mario then went back to his writing. Poem after poem, and short stories, too. He kept writing even when he was not sure if they could eventually be published at all. Most Chinese writers were still in prison and we had no contact with our friends and family back in the home country. Our parents did not know where we were. We decided at this time to have a second child.

MY FIRST pregnancy was a rather difficult one. Having married young and having been away from my mother who had no inkling at all that I was in China, and could not be with us, I depended a lot on Mario. Fortunately, our colleagues in the Radio were all very helpful, protective and caring. After my threatened miscarriage, I was given a long rest at home and a very light work load.

Our first winter seemed to be a never-ending season of overcast skies punctuated by the peeping of the sun every once in a while. Then came the first snow in our life. Snow was not only a most beautiful sight in winter. Its whiteness covered the coal-blackened smokestacks, the dusty red bricks, the withered leafless trees, the pavements sullied by frozen spit. It also brought moisture to the otherwise very dry and piercingly cold air. It was, in a way, a harbinger of spring. I was delighted to see my first snow. Mario, meanwhile, remained in bed with his *ganmao*.

Spring came suddenly in mid-April. In almost just one day, the apple, plum and peach trees sprang forth their white and pink blossoms, the willow trees their delicate fronds and the walnut trees their wormlike buds. It was on such a day that I was brought to the hospital by our non-too-proletarian chauffeur-driven limousine after I found a stain in my underwear. As it was my first experience in childbirth, I did not realize the first signs of my labor pangs.

The Miclat family in Hong Kong, 1985

I went through long and tedious labor pains from morning till night and beyond. It was a continuation of the arduous pregnancy I have gone through. At dawn the following day, Mario was asked by the doctor to choose whom he would want saved first. He was grief-stricken. I was whisked to the X-ray room to determine the position of the baby. A battery of specialists, some recalled from the labor stint in the countryside, was tasked to get ready for a Caesarian operation. Their discussions about my situation, complete with the recitations of quotations from Chairman Mao, seemed endless to me.

Mario kept me company and so did our interpreter who was translating what the doctors were saying. My eyes were bloodshot with lack of sleep, and all I wanted was to get over and done with it.

When I heard that I was to be operated on, something inside me ticked. In a short while, the doctors were surprised that the birth opening was such that I must be brought to the delivery room. Mario was holding my hand but he was not allowed inside the delivery room. The practice of a husband witnessing childbirth was still anathema to the Chinese. I would learn about the Lamaze method of childbirth only after I had given birth to my two daughters. But I did use the method of proper breathing and right timing and with shouts of encouragement from the interpreter, I brought forth Maningning into the world at 9:45 a.m. on the 15th day of April. It was a normal delivery. The tremendous pain I had suffered brought me now not tears of bitterness, but only happiness and relief. Later, Mario and I would make fun of the fact that the date was also the birthday of an Asian who was to be greater than Mao, Lenin, and all other communist icons combined, none other than the North Korean theocrat, Kim Il Sung. After the Cultural Revolution, we would learn that some Southeast Asian countries celebrate the date as the birthday of Gautama Buddha. No wonder all the flowers bloom on this day.

Mario was beside himself with joy upon seeing me and our daughter both well and doing good. His eyes were moist at the sight of the frail and tiny five-and-a-half pound baby girl sucking her first drops of milk from her mother's breast. In China, they starved new-born babies for 24 hours before they were fed the mother's colostrum.

My second baby, Banaue, who came after seven years had a different story altogether. We were no longer much the well-protected state guests we were years earlier. We had learned the language and could go to different places by our happy selves without needing interpreters and guides. We had already adjusted to China's climate, food and way of life. It was also the time when the cultural revolution had ended, if only officially, following the death of Mao.

As in the birth of our firstborn, Mario was not allowed inside the delivery room. He told the doctor it was right for him to wait at the lobby, since he had already dismissed the driver and the car. But the doctor told him to go back to work, saying I was not about to give birth any time soon. It was twelve noon and the Chinese religiously have their lunch at that time. It was the most cruel month and the hottest week in China's summer. Nobody attended to me even as I was already shouting at the top of my voice for assistance. I thought I could by then communicate without the help of an interpreter.

Banaue was conceived after our month-long vacation in the exclusive Badaguan seaside resort of Qingdao (Tsingtao), Shandong. Mario and I, together with Maningning had gone there to recuperate from primary complex which he in no time transmitted to me when he came home with it from the country. The balmy sea breeze and the fresh produce from the ocean invigorated us and we went back to Beijing fully charged and healthy once again.

The pregnancy was not as difficult as the first, or I must say, was not difficult at all, but I felt the pain more, and the heartache even more so, because of the indifference of the attending physician. Mario seemed so far away because he heeded the doctor's order and went back to his office that Saturday, July 21, 1979. He would dash back to the hospital upon receiving the call that he had another baby girl.

As there had been a change in China's leadership calling for liberalization and reforms, we reiterated our request to live a more or less normal lifestyle away from the exclusive eighteen villas. We thought we owe it to our Maningning and our new baby, Banaue, to leave the confines of *Shibasuo*. We finally lived a semblance of normal life in *Zhuanjialou* or Foreign Experts' Building, an enclave of foreigners working at Radio Peking. There, our two children were able to make friends with other children easily.

Although *Zhuanjialou* was also guarded by the PLA, outsiders were allowed in upon registration at the gate. It was a walking distance to the office and surrounded by Chinese apartments. We no longer needed our chauffeured limousine. We were freer to take public transport and could bike around, too.

Foreign experts coming from Turkey, England, Sri Lanka, Thailand, India, Pakistan, Malaysia, Indonesia, Laos, Brazil, Bolivia, Portugal, Japan, Guinea and many other countries lived like a big family. We ate in the same cavernous canteen, partaking of the same kind of food every same day of the week, year in year out. Even so, we were happy that life was more normal than in *Shibasuo*.

In this mini-United Nations of sorts, we got into real friendship with some of the foreigners which we keep up to now. Our Turkish friend, Maci, who's married to Yvonne from England, taught Mario the rudiments of photography. Together, they would venture out to take photos and develop the negatives in the improvised dark room utilizing our bathroom. Meanwhile, Yvonne and I would have our own way of baking cookies, cakes and pies using a makeshift oven, again in the bathroom since our flat is hotel-style and we don't have a kitchen. The four of us would bike together exploring *hutong* or sidestreets, museums, antique shops, and small eateries in the nooks and crannies of Beijing. Their daughter and our daughters including the other *Zhuanjialou* kids, multi-racial kids—brown, yellow, white and black—spoke, played and quarrelled in one and the same language: Chinese.

MARIO GREW up in a big family, the fourth in a brood of seven. He had many happy memories of his childhood with discipline and sense of responsibility taught to them at an early age. As I have said, I was first attracted to him by his intelligence and kindness. I would, of course, know him better later on. He was very open about his feelings and very passionate about the things he believed in. Others misjudge him as being inflexible, but even this becomes positive at times. He could also be very temperamental, a trait I would like to attribute to his intense artistic inclinations and which our two daughters also possess.

Our Chinese colleagues who were schooled in the traditional concepts told us that I should not read after giving birth as my eyesight would be damaged irreparably. What Mario did was to read to me religiously after he came back from work each day. As we did not want to get help to take care of the baby, we did everything ourselves. Mario learned to change diapers. At first, he was holding the soiled diapers with his fingers but in no time, he became so adept at washing them in the bath tub that he was even better than me.

When one of the babies developed a colic and cried without letup, he would put her to sleep by resting the baby face down on his chest while he was lying flat face up. This always did the trick and the baby would sleep like an angel. We were finally convinced by the Chinese to take an *aiyi* (amah) to help us with our first, then the second baby. But we decided to have their cradles brought to our room at night, instead of making them stay in their own nursery. This so they could be brought up the Filipino way.

Mario forever doted on his children. He never underestimated the kids. He talked to them as equals but disciplining them also in the process. He never embarrassed them if they did something to be embarrassed about. He had a great way of making them feel they could be what they wanted to be.

Maningning was two months old when he came home from a trip to Shanghai. He brought her a jumping toy dog mechanically playing with a ball. He thought that the baby could already play with it and was disappointed to see that she was still too small to appreciate it. A precocious child, Maningning learned to speak even before she could walk and grew up so gentle in her ways. Mario and I made it a point to be fair with the two children. What we did for Maningning, we also did for Banaue. We spoke to them in our language and made sure that they learned it beside Chinese which they knew as a matter of course, being surrounded by the Chinese including their Chinese amah.

Mario recorded both the children's first utterances, the tape of which is still a source of delight and enjoyment to us now that Maningning is already a young professional having finished her bachelor in fine arts course and working as a freelance artist and as an occasional Chinese interpreter and writer. Banaue meanwhile is taking up theater arts. With Banaue we realized there is no single formula in bringing up children. Banaue started walking earlier than her age group and would climb sofas, tables and fences when others were just starting to learn their first steps.

THE RIGID do's and don'ts, must's and musn'ts of the China cultural revolution discouraged creativity in general. Mario could not find himself writing fiction based solely on political orthodoxy and CCP-imposed formulas. I saw him write poems surreptitiously every once in a while, but most of his time was spent in Radio Peking work. He did a lot of translation work, mostly classics in political economy, as well as of Chinese, Vietnamese and Russian fiction.

His short story, *"Sang Araw ng Paghihintay"* was written in 1982 when he was feeling very depressed, not only about our prolonged exile in China but mostly also about martial law in the Philippines. It was a gloomy and foreboding piece of Kafkaesque fiction. "Pinoy Odyssey" on the other hand is an unconventional, if playful account reminescent of a colorful Philippine collage, hitting the very essence of Filipino sensibility right at its mark.

Shock and disbelief engulfed us when we heard about Ninoy Aquino's assassination. Mario's "The Assassination of a Citizen" was inspired by that single dastardly act of cowardice which galvanized the whole Filipino nation into action. He entered the manuscript in *Asiaweek's* literary contest. Although it did not win the major award, it was cited as one of the ten best.

His experiences living in a commune in the countryside amidst political uncertainties is the subject of "Antonio and His China Wall." It later won a Palanca Award for short story in 1986-87. He garnered the Grand Prize in the Gawad CCP para sa Panitikan for his *"Ang*

The Miclat family in Manila, 1987

Rebolusyon Ay Katotohanan," a short story written after we finally returned home to the Philippines.

MARIO IS very committed to his writing craft. He is so passionate about his creative work and nobody, not even me, dares disturb him when he's into his nocturnal bouts with his Muse.

Coming home in 1986 right after the EDSA revolution, I found myself looking for a job while Mario took the post offered to him as instructor at the U.P. Asian Center. We would enter another phase of life.

Mario went on to teach and handle administrative work as college secretary and assistant to the dean for administration of the Asian Center while doing his M.A. in Asian Studies. After finishing his M.A., I prodded him to work for a Ph.D. We had an unwritten understanding that I would look for a job that could sustain us, while he would go on writing and teaching, making do with the meager salary that he gets from the State University. It was therefore a boon when he got a grant from the PHP Matsushita to finish his Ph.D.

Mario and I have gone through a lot. We have suffered emotionally in an alien country, yet we also hurt somewhat when we left that alien land for home. In China, we spent the most creative and best years of our life, our youth. It was there where sprang the two most wonderful kids who brought enormous happiness to our wearied souls. Through it all, we struggled, we matured, we learned, and we survived.

Nowadays, each member of the family has some project or another, and it is difficult to get hold of the computer at home. Like Mario, Maningning is also into writing, and so is Banaue. I forever find small pieces of paper in Mario's pants or shirts with a word or a phrase which I later see in his stories or poems, like seeds germinating into a treasure trove of words and ideas. I look at the two girls and see their father's creative genes in them. Their genes sure tell a story. But that is yet another story.

ONE DECEMBER DAY, I attended a reunion of former martial law political detainees and activists. It was a potluck dinner. I thought of bringing something I have not cooked for ten years since arriving in the Philippines. People swore they loved the taste of the dessert I prepared. I smiled. It was apple pie, and it could have been made of small green Peking apples.

Preciosa S. Soliven
Commander-in-Chief

On June 1997, Max and I celebrated our 40th wedding anniversary. Max used to refer to himself as a cradle-snatcher because I was 17 when he first met me. That remained my identity as a fledgling housewife between 1957-1967. After I established and developed the O.B. Montessori school into several branches between 1967-1976, he referred to me as "my commander". But during martial law when he lost his job, he introduced me as "my bread winner". Today, he prefers to identify me as "wife number one," specially when he introduces me to businessmen and diplomats.

He is fond of teasing me, recalling to others that "Precious went to my house to meet me." It was at a New Year's Eve barn dance party organized by Max's mother, Pelagia V. Soliven, and Fr. Lynch, S.J. for the Square Dance Club.

Earlier that day, Max's sisters Augie, Tessa and Ethel, were busy preparing their patio and house for about

Max and Precious with youngest daughter Sara

60 SDC members. Augie revealed to me a few years ago that they were teasing Max, "You better take time off (as night editor of the *Manila Chronicle*, covering the police beat) and come home tonight so you can meet Precious!" Max was intrigued by the name and thus, dropped by while we were promenading and do-si-doing away merrily.

"WHO'S THAT handsome gentleman with a pipe, reading in the library?" I asked Pepot Enriquez. "That's Max. Let me introduce you." Max's bright and friendly smile made my heart skip. (I felt guilty since I had a steady boyfriend, also a senior college student from Ateneo.) Max was so down-to-earth and funny.

Noticing a white ring mark on his finger, I inquired, "Where's your college ring?"

"It will soon come back.", he winked. "I just broke up with my girlfriend from Negros...I should be banging my head against the wall, but I am amazed that I don't feel like it."

Whew! Was I relieved. Then, practicing all tips I frequently

Precious with "Snow White's dwarves" in her weekly TV show, *Montessori for Everyone*

read on "how to be charming and interesting " I interviewed him about his work. I listened enraptured and wished we could continue getting acquainted even after the party.

I found myself saying, "Soon, we shall have our Junior-Senior Prom...and I have no date."

Right away, Max picked up and said, "I'd be very happy to be your escort. What's the attire?" A formal suit, I answered.

Then I wondered aloud, "What will you do when the New Year breaks in?"

He said, "Oh poor me, I'll be stuck in Precinct No. 4 in Isaac Peral (U.N. Avenue). I do the police beat."

"I live in Singalong," I said, "It's not far away. Perhaps I can send you Mama's nice sandwiches."

"That would be most welcome.", he replied. All the time I thought we were merely teasing each other, but to my surprise, he meant everything.

Later, he confided to me that he waited at Precinct No. 4 until dawn break and no sandwiches arrived. He also had a suit made for our Junior-Senior Prom in March, but to his disappointment, I never followed up the invitation. The *nuncio* banned all junior-senior proms that year.

Meantime, I attended another New Year's party with my steady boyfriend. Bobby must have sensed that my attention was nowhere and definitely away from him. He took me home early.

THE COURTSHIP style in the '50s compared to the practice today is vastly different. It was customary then to entertain several admirers. They came usually accompanied by gangmates to call on their favorite girl during weekends. In the mid-seventies, when my daughters were in high school, the custom was to have one special "boyfriend" or "girlfriend" right away. I used to encourage my daughters to let their friends come over to the house before they eventually choose a steady. They said that it is not customary as in my days.

Neither would they hear of having a relative to chaperone them on single dates. Dating as foursome with friends was more acceptable.

We were very much influenced by both the nuns at St. Scholastica's College and Hollywood. I had an Audrey Hepburn, haircut plus bangs. Pastel-colored organdie dresses with ruffles and petticoats were in fashion a la Debbie Reynolds, Ann Blythe or Grace Kelly. To me, courtship time was by appointment from 4:00 to 6:00 p.m. A girl went to parties in groups, usually with gangmates — so with the boys. Girls were given the courtesy to sit down around the dance floor while the gentlemen ogled them. This allowed a young man to spot easily the girls he would prefer to dance with. A few girls had their boyfriends with whom they danced the whole night. Chaperoning on single dates was often practiced.

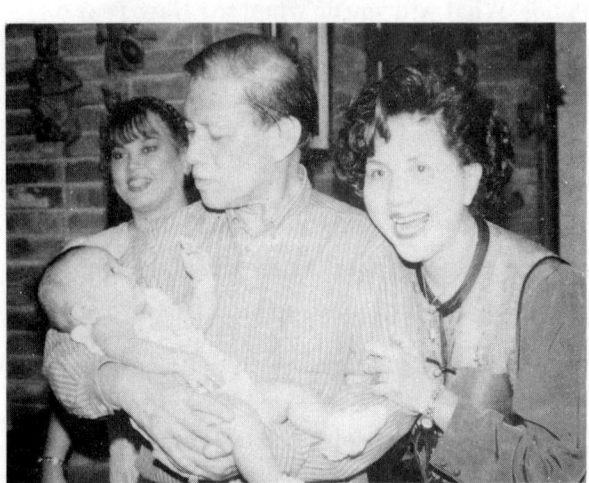
Max and Precious with daughter Marinella Pascual and one of her three children, Guinevere

SINCE NEW Year, I did not receive calls from Max. By the Feast of the Three Kings, Bobby was due to see me. Max suddenly called up asking if he could see me right away. Calculating that he must come after Bobby, I told him to come at 6:00 in the evening. Bobby felt I was in a hurry to let him go. I explained in my immature way that Max Soliven wanted to see me about something. Bobby got mad and promptly asked back his school ring. I did not argue anymore and handed it to him. I felt lighter and relieved. I no longer felt guilty.

In a few minutes, Max arrived. Holding an issue of *The Manila*

Chronicle folded on the editorial columnists' page, he started to explain, "I would like to apologize for this item written by our senior writer and columnist: 'Max Soliven, who has just lost his girl from Negros, is now in hot pursuit of a girl from Bulacan.'" Perhaps an older girl would have objected being gossiped about specially since there has been no courtship, but I was not that mature. In my naivete, I even welcomed the write-up for it gave Max the excuse to begin courting me.

ANOTHER PLEASED member of the family was my Lolo Manuel. When my father was killed by the Japanese, we transferred to Lolo's house in Singalong. After the war, when Manila was heavily bombed, the Americans bulldozed and cleared up the ruins between San Andres, Singalong and Herran (now Pedro Gil). Without our knowing it, our house in Singalong was one of the few which remained; Max's residence was on the Herran side across this huge empty site which was an American camp.

Lolo Manuel, who had run for councilor in Manila, was always interested in politics. He had heard so much and admired Max's father—Diputado Benito Soliven of Ilocos Sur. "A brave man who lost his life in Bataan, a brilliant lawyer...a hero of our country," Lolo Manuel would eulogize Max's father.

Thus, every weekend, Lolo looked forward to Max's visit. He called him Don Maximo, and Max responded well to this attention at the same time reviewing his Spanish since Lolo preferred to converse with him in Spanish. Due to this, Max has to look in his archive of information about how my Lolo, as a major, fought both in the Spanish and American wars. He even knows about the deep scars inflicted on Lolo during the Siege of Guadalupe.

MAX BEGAN courting me intensely. Every night, he would call.

That summer, I went to Baguio and, later, to Gingoog, near Cagayan de Oro in Mindanao, where my cousin invited me to the town fiesta. I joined my auntie's family in Aurora Hill in a rented cottage. The first morning, lo and behold, *The Manila Chronicle* van drove up to the hill and delivered a letter to me from Max. Rod Reyes was the "postman".

FINALLY, IT was time to leave for Gingoog. This proved to be quite exciting—involving an overnight island boat trip. My Aunt Plicia, an old maid who used to bring us to long vacations in the Visayas, saw me off with my mother. Pretty soon, Max also arrived. He did not want me to go, he said, specially since he could not follow.

An incredible thing happened.

As the boat shook, we all swayed with it. Max, a gentleman, held my elbow to steady me. Suddenly, someone snapped, "Filipino custom, no touch!" It was Aunt Plicia, still over-protective.

I saw Max's face red and furious. I didn't know he has a temper. How he controlled himself from screaming was incredible.

During the fiesta, there was a dance practically every night. On the main night, the traditional search for the fiesta queen was held. I won it against a beauty from Butuan.

AFTER I turned 18, Max proposed to me. He wanted to get married soon, but agreed to wait patiently until I graduated. He gave me a diamond engagement ring which his mother got engaged with. Since it was my senior year as Bachelor of Arts (Nutrition) major in St. Scholastica's College in Leon Guinto Street (formerly Pennsylvania), I asked him to type for me a 250-page nutrition case study of how balanced the students' meals are at the PNU school canteen. He readily worked on it, claiming that he had typed a medical thesis a few years back.

I tried Max's patience frequently because I had the bad habit of making Max wait everytime we'd go out. One time, I made him wait at the Aguinaldo's department store for an hour. When I arrived, he snapped, "This is too much. We are incompatible. We better break up." But I took this moment calmly and just smiled back and we were on again.

A romantic, Max tried everything to please me. Not a day passed without Max giving me a call. On weekends, we would see movies and take *meriendas* at Aristocrat at Roxas Boulevard. His favorite was *mami* and *siopao* at Ma Mon Luk. Many other young ladies were having crushes on him. Lecturing at St. Theresa's College and Far Eastern University, he would complain of female students sitting on the front row, just staring at him dreamily. To show me off occasionally, he would let me substitute in his classes to proctor his exams.

Even with his additional income from lecturing, his salary from *Manila Times*, where he transferred as Assistant Business Editor, was quite modest. However, he was confident we could build our own house, borrowing from RFC. (We built a two-bedroom house as planned on my in-laws' lot in Herran.) For 10 years, I would pay P150 monthly for the loan. Max would show me his bank book, now and then.

I GUESS, because he thought me young and inexperienced, Max did all the wedding preparations although he allowed me to follow my personal preferences. Besides he, as the Filipino groom, had to shoulder the major expenses.

The first consideration was the number of guests. Then the hotel venue for the reception. He also let me choose and order my wedding gown, as well as that for my sister as maid of honor, and for the bridesmaids and flower girls.

My parish church, St. Anthony's at Singalong had involved me in their activities in the Legion of Mary; hence, the nuptial mass had to be celebrated there. Raul Manglapus, his uncle Sixto Brillante, and my college teachers Dr. Juan Salcedo and Dr. Intengan, were the sponsors. Mayor Arsenio Lacson, a close friend, dropped by the church briefly and also showed up at the reception.

Again, Max made the best arrangements. With 150 guests, half and half for both our families and relatives, we held our wedding reception after the mass with breakfast at the Champagne Room of the Manila Hotel. He was rather harried since Chat Peypoch, who did our portraits for the photo album right after the mass, made the *ninongs* and guests wait.

Of our wedding gifts, the bonanza gift was a honeymoon trip to Hong Kong, courtesy of Philippine Airlines. They were having their inaugural flight to Hong Kong on our wedding day. The hotel accommodation and *baon* for four days were the combined gifts of businessmen for their favorite young journalist. In addition, Max had so many other friends who we met in Hong Kong and insisted on taking us out.

As a teenage bride in Hong Kong, I found myself imagining that we were like the stars of *Love Is A Many Splendored Thing*, Bill Holden and Jennifer Jones and therefore should follow the footsteps of these very romantic stars as they were filmed in Hong Kong. Luckily, the *Manila Times* man in Hong Kong was Harvey Liang—ever so knowledgeable about the nooks and crannies of Hong Kong and ever so patient.

Max and Precious Soliven with Veronica Pedrosa at CNN Atlanta

MAX BUILT our two-bedroom house behind the family house in Herran. As a Nutrition major, I hosted small dinners for Max and journalist friends. He was very proud of our home and my cooking.

Mama Pelagia was a very friendly and thoughtful mother-in-law. In two years, Max and I moved to Saigon where he worked with Vietnam Presse during President Ngo Dich Diem's administration. A French, Australian, British and Ceylonese journalist worked with Max to write a guidebook for Vietnamese journalists. (When Max's younger brothers married, they started life in our house in Herran.) I got used to the military state of the country. Every block had a soldier standing guard with an *uzi* machine gun. The daily newspaper had empty spaces where a censored article had been deleted.

A small community of Filipino engineers lived in Saigon, some with their families. The first lady ambassador of the Philippines, social philanthropist Doña Trinidad Legarda, served this community. Well-poised, intelligent and beautiful, Ambassador Legarda in her elegant Philippine *terno* was popular in the diplomatic circle. So impressed and proud of this lady, I decided to write an article about her for *Graphic Magazine*.

This was my first try at writing. Max encouraged me, but was a little anxious though. Living in Saigon provided me materials to write more articles, and allowed me to experience other worlds: Vietnamese and French cultures. Chic French ladies, some of them *mestizas*, were still residing in the city. At the nearby beach, Cap St. Jacques, they wore bikinis. Our first car was a second-hand British Hillman. I learned to drive in Saigon. Max was chaffeured every morning in a Citroen French car to office. Although we brought Sayong, our housekeeper, to Saigon, we had to hire Thuy, a Vietnamese who spoke colloquial French. I also learned to cook some Vietnamese recipes like imperial pate and shrimp on sugar sticks.

Mama Pelagia stayed with us a few years. Since there were no babies yet, I began to teach. English-speaking teachers were scarce. I got two jobs: in a primary Vietnam school near the house and a Jesuit Chinese school in Cholon or China town.

THE MAJOR decisions in our lives were about Max's shifting from one newspaper to another. When we got married, the first career shift occurred. Max, who received an award for the expose "The Truth About American Advisers in the Philippines" written for *Manila Chronicle,* joined the *Manila Times.* He was under two great editors, Joe Bautista and Dave Boguslav. Chino Roces and Bibilo Prieto took him under their wing. Max wrote another series on the lumber racket in the Philippines. These front-paged articles alerted the Japanese *Gaimushu* since Japan was anxious to rebuild their war-damaged relationship with the Philippines. Incisive character studies of major politicians from the Magsaysay, Garcia and Macapagal administrations, including the controversial Namarco deals, won him the Ten Outstanding Young Men or TOYM award sponsored by Caltex. Ninoy Aquino, Flash Elorde and Benito Legarda also received the TOYM the same time Max did.

Eventually, he was asked by Harry Stonehill to become publisher of the *Evening News.* He was then 29 years old. For the following two years, the circulation of the paper zoomed from number six to number two, next to the top paper, *The Manila Times.* It was the first three-edition newspaper in the country. Among his reporters were Louie Beltran, Julie Yap Daza, Minnie Narciso, Sonny Valencia, Manny Benitez, Jake Clave, and Neal Cruz.

When controversy blew up which revealed Stonehill bribing many politicians from the Presidency down to Congress, Max resigned from *The Evening News.* It was a nerve-wracking period. Therefore, the Kissinger grant in Harvard provided a much-needed change. Max joined a select group of professionals from all over the world to spend one summer with Henry Kissinger, Dean of International Relations in Harvard University in Cambridge, Massachusetts. I joined Max and travelled to the United States for the first time.

On the way back, Max decided to travel leisurely through Europe saying, "We shall never have this chance again." So for almost ten months, we looked up his Harvard classmates in London, France, Italy and Germany. We stayed longer with "bachelor" Ambassador Mel Aquino in the embassy residence in Bonn. We travelled using the new Arthur Frommer's *$5 A Day in Europe.*

FORESEEING a coup d'etat, Max did not renew his contract. We returned to Manila. While he was publisher of *The Evening News*, I worked half-day at Telly Albert Zulueta's Pre-School in San Lorenzo Village, Makati. I handled the four-year olds of different nationalities. One of them, Patrick, tried to outsmart me and almost succeeded. An extremely intelligent child, he easily got bored playing dollhouse, easel painting, cutting and pasting, etc. He preferred running and playing in the yard. After the half-hour recess, he would clown on the table top. His classmates would heartily applaud. Then he would call out, *"Let's go!"* Off the table he would jump and run out for a second recess with all the kids following him, leaving me all by myself.

Finally, I requested Mrs. Zulueta to transfer him to another class. In two weeks, I was surprised to see him so docile and obedient. Silently, he worked on geography puzzle maps and arithmetic memorization charts. He thoroughly enjoyed the Montessori class of our Swiss teacher, Elsbeth Graemigher.

Patrick had a superior I.Q. He could be challenged only when occupied with interesting work. This experience converted me to the Montessori system. I also concluded that pre-schoolers are capable of doing more challenging activities than mere play.

I RESIGNED from the San Lorenzo Pre-School in 1964. Four years of enriching training and experience working with pre-schoolers and writing their weekly individual anecdotal records was preparing me for my professional Montessori training in Europe.

Before this happened, I was offered to organize pre-schools for the first major relocation of squatters. Three thousand families inhabiting the historical walls of the Spanish port of Intramuros were being transferred to the suburbs of Sapang Palay, Bulacan. Oscar Arellano, president of Operation Brotherhood International (OBI), took charge of 300 families.

An OBI team of doctors, nurses, social workers, food technologists and agronomists was replicated for the Philippines, a counterpart of the eight-year old Filipino teams servicing then in the rehabilitation of Vietnam and Laos. Unlike the government municipal and health officials, the OBI team worked almost 24 hours a day. In fact, they lived at the site. Providing a pre-school for their very young children raised so much hope for these "refugees".

Ambassador Rubino of Italy was touched with my work of training the nurses and food technologists to do part-time teaching at the pre-schools. He offered me a scholarship in Italy. All along, Max backed me up in my work, knowing fully well how I loved working with children. I stayed an extra full term to review the course in English on a British Council grant in London.

PARADOXICALLY, it was at this period when we had our first child, Rachelle. Other husbands would not have allowed their wives to leave since the baby was just on the crawling stage. But Max was happy for my opportunity to study and live abroad. Having experienced it, he did not want to deny me this golden opportunity.

"Let me baby-sit for Rachelle." And baby-sit he did. At times, he would bring Rachelle to the newsmen's breakfast meeting at Country Bake Shop or to cocktail parties. The nursemaid would usually follow. Three grandmothers and a grand aunt, including young uncles and aunts, almost spoiled Rachelle.

By 1966, when Ferdinand Marcos became President, Elizabeth Marcos was my guardian in Rome. As press attache of the Philippine Embassy, she volunteered to Max that she would look after me. That was from 1964 to 1966. When I returned to organize the first O.B. Montessori school right beside the OBI office at Syquia Apartments in M.H. del Pilar, I myself was the teacher. Twenty pupils including Oscar Arellano's grandchildren (Jackie and Gabby Concepcion), my nephews, my nieces, Kokoy Romualdez's boys, Tony Ayala's two oldest sons, Minister Minford's son Leslie, and others were among my students. The press women were impressed by the children's concentration on Geography, Botany, Zoology, Math and Geometry. They preferred work to play. The first one to do Montessori laundry was Nora Daza's daughter, Nina. The Montessori laundry consisted of 13 steps. Table setting with breakable plates and linen tablecloth was a favorite chore. Georgie Martel loved ironing but absent-mindedly burned a line on his cheek with the tiny Italian iron. The skin puffed but subsided overnight.

In 1969 to 1970, I did the advanced elementary school course at the Centro Montessori Internazionale at Bergamo, Italy. Then, I went back to Manila to start the O.B. Montessori grade school.

SINCE IT was difficult to explain what the Montessori system of education is about and to arrest the mushrooming of false Montessori pre-schools, I decided to present a Montessori TV show which could inform and demonstrate to both parents and educators the distinction between the traditional and the true Montessori system of child guidance.

This was not easy.

I hand-carried my proposal to Geny Lopez, the chairman of the most popular TV station in the country, ABS-CBN. All their programs could beam to most provinces of the Philippines.

By coincidence, ABS-CBN also wanted Max to do a weekly evening interview program. Max was back at *The Manila Times* writing, "A Word Edgewise," daily.

Geny, with Jake Almeda Lopez, was convinced. I brought a whole classroom filled with Montessori apparata. Two senior teachers and

Max and Precious Soliven at the Sunburst magazine office. Mrs. Soliven was a contributing editor specializing in food articles.

eight pre-schoolers chosen weekly from each of the four O.B. Montessori schools helped demonstrate Practical Life exercises in Care of the Person and Environment, Sensorial Education, language, Math and Cultural Arts. Every month, I featured a musical. Ambassadors' wives were presented during Christmas with their multinational community events. The show created a wave of enthusiasm. All over the country, the "new children" and the "new teacher" were being discovered. My program became 17th of 400 weekly TV shows.

By September 21, 1972, all television studios, radio stations and newspapers were shut down. President Ferdinand Marcos declared Martial Law. It was right after Max exposed in his show, *"Impact",* Operation Sagittarius. Instead of featuring then Secretary of Defense Fidel Ramos, Ninoy Aquino came on live, giving details of the coming Martial Law.

Max and Ninoy were arrested with Chino Roces, Teddy Locsin, one labor judge, two Constitutional Convention delegates, Soc Rodrigo and Senator Pepe Diokno. Secretary Fidel Ramos assured Max that everything would be all right.

Meantime, I continued with my school work. Max was released after 80 days in early December. Noble Soriano made him editor of an international magazine, *Sunburst.* He was still under house arrest and could not leave the country until after 1977. By 1975, he was allowed to write a monthly column for *Sunburst* entitled, "In This Corner."

DURING THE martial law years of 1973 and 1983, Max could not be involved in any kind of newspapers due to censorship. However, he went into magazine publication. *Sunburst* and, later, *Manila* magazine, were glossy colored magazines featuring beautiful Filipino ladies and girls on the cover and the latest pictorial stories gathered from the major cities of the country.

Meantime, the Marcos administration did not touch my O.B. Montessori school management. By 1972, my Montessori weekly TV show, like many ABS-CBN TV programs, were closed up but due to my show's popularity, there was a phenomenal mushrooming of false Montessori pre-schools.

DECS-NCR Director Nilo Rosas had to intervene. He co-sponsored a seminar entitled, "Upgrading Quality Montessori Pre-Schools Through Mutual Cooperation" for pre-school entrepreneurs. The solution had to be the putting up of the O.B. Montessori College to be able to give a degree course, Bachelor of Elementary Education major in Montessori Pre-School Teaching and Management.

By 1981, when the O.B. Montessori Professional High School was launched, we initiated our outreach program for underprivileged children.

In collaboration with the National Housing Authority (NHA), using the Montessori pre-school curriculum which I re-programmed to be affordable, we acquired rent-free barangay halls and teacher college trainees endowed by eight improved slum zones and set up between 1983 to 1993 eight Montessori pre-schools I identified as *"Pagsasarili."*

By 1984, I experimented with the Pagsasarili Literacy program for the village mothers of Cadiz. Under the auspices of Mayor Rowena

Guanzon and planter Punay Kabayao Fernandez, I trained 21 plantation mother trainees. Since Montessori pre-schooling would be unaffordable and difficult to monitor in the provinces, I trained the mothers themselves, using the system and a post-literacy program. I foresaw that this would lead to a retraining of these mothers eventually as Pagsasarili Pre-School Teachers.

BEFORE THE Marcoses were ousted, the public had to be fully prepared for regaining liberty from a dictatorship. Max was invited to publish the *Inquirer*, a new daily. Max accepted and went to work right away in the dingy and dark office Betty Go-Belmonte set up at Port Area on the corner of 13th Street and Railroad Street. He asked Louie Beltran, Letty Jimenez-Magsanoc and Art Borjal to join him. He firmly believed that the new President should revolutionize the government and cut off completely all Marcosian policies and practice. But as time went on, Ninoy's observation that whoever succeeds Marcos will likely fail was coming true for he has almost destroyed our liberty.

The *Inquirer* helped liberate the Filipino spirit from the stupor of dictatorship. Max's column, "A Word Edgewise," was sought after.

When Corazon Aquino became President, I was asked by the Foreign Affairs Minister Salvador Laurel to represent the Philippines in the highest board of UNESCO, the *conseil executif* in Paris. Retired Prime Ministers, cabinet members and well-known educators and social scientists representing Member States of the world, now totalling 171, made up the prestigious group.

As one of four women representatives, I found myself frequently raising the Montessori ideals in education. Ambassador Wagner from Brazil recalled that Dr. Maria Montessori was acknowledged highly by UNESCO when it was just founded in 1946 until she died in 1952. Dr. Montessori wrote the first Declaration of Children's Rights which was adapted by the UNESCO.

The Director-General then of UNESCO at the time was the Senegalese Amathar M'Bow. The global crusade for Eradication of Illiteracy was the major goal. Accessing good education to the less privileged, the juvenile and adult drop-outs and rural women was another major project.

My demonstration of the Pagsasarili Pre-School using the multinational pre-school dependents was highly appreciated by Mr. M'Bow and the Secretariat. By 1993, the project, twined with Pagsasarili Mothercraft, won one of the International Literacy Awards.

AS CHAIRMAN of the Operation Brotherhood Montessori Center, Inc. Board, Max and I, as school president, feel very grateful for the blessings that come from the our establishment the O.B. Montessori schools for 4,600 pre-schoolers, graders, high school and college students in Metro Manila, Pampanga and Zambales.

Our marriage has blended with our writing and teaching concerns very well.

"But let all those that put their trust in thee rejoice... For thou, Lord, will bless the righteous; with favor wilt thou compass him as with a shield." (Psalms 4: 11-12)

About the Wives

MERCY RIVERA ABAD does a balancing act running TRENDS-MBL (a marketing company); managing a poet-professor's household; and being mother to Cyan, Cybele, David and Diego. She loves cooking and playing classical guitar. She finds Tai Chi and doing the laundry great ways to relax.

CONCEPCION REYNOSO ANGELES is very supportive of poet-husband Carlos. The couple is enjoying life in La Puente, California where they live and where Connie is active in parish work.

ROSE MARIE BAUTISTA is Director of the School of Design and Arts in De La Salle University (DLSU)-College of St. Benilde. She also teaches at the Philippine School of Interior Design. Rose Marie is doting grandmother to two wonderful kids, Mira and Miguel. Husband Cirilo teaches at DLSU and writes for the *Manila Bulletin*.

LINDA TY-CASPER lives in a "writer's paradise" with husband Len in Saxonville, Massachusetts. Linda, a lawyer-turned-writer has written numerous novels in English and has received awards for her outstanding works.

ROSALINA ICBAN-CASTRO taught literature before she retired. She wrote a book on Pampanga literature and articles about her travels around the world with her husband. She was already a widow when she wrote the essay in this anthology. She passed away in 1998 and left a beautiful garden and lovely paintings behind.

REMEDIOS CALMA CRUZ is an executive at China Banking Corporation. She is finishing her doctorate in Business Administration at DLSU. She and husband Isagani are proud parents of two pretty young women.

JUNE POTICAR-DALISAY is a woman of many talents. Beng, as she is fondly called by friends, is a painter, graphic designer, restorer/conservator of documents and paintings, and acupuncturist. Her numerous watercolors have already been exhibited and have been used on book covers.

JOY VIERNES ENRIQUEZ lives with her husband Tony in Cagayan de Oro. An accomplished pianist, she teaches at Xavier University and is curator of the Xavier Museum.

NARITA MANUEL GONZALEZ was born in Zamboanga. She earned her B.S.E. and M.H.E. degrees from the University of the Philippines (U.P.) and her M.S. from California State University, Hayward. She recently lost her husband of 57 years, N.V.M., and is trying hard to adjust to being a widow. She keeps busy writing and editing. She hopes to finish a children's book dedicated to N.V.M. entitled *Once Upon a Garden, Campus Flowers, Weeds and Trees*.

JULITA QUIMING HUFANA has been working as a nurse all her married life. She and husband Alex live in California.

EDNA MAY OBIEN-LANDICHO is deeply involved in the academe, theater, movies, television, and literature. An award-winning playwright, she has co-authored several children's books and has written scripts for TV. She is a theater director, actress and professor in speech communication and theater arts at U.P. Diliman.

ALMA CRUZ MICLAT is Assistant Vice-President for Sales and Marketing of Data Center Design Corporation. She took up Chemical Engineering at U.P.; Chinese Language and Literature under Liu Dazhao of the Foreign Experts' Bureau of the Ministry of Radio, Film and Television. She and husband Mario have two daughters: writer and painter Maningning and theater student and actress Banaue.

PRECIOSA S. SOLIVEN is president and training director of the four O.B. Montessori schools and the new College in Manila and 23 outreach Pagsasarili Literacy schools for village mothers and children. She was Executive Board Member of UNESCO-Paris from 1986-1987 and is currently UNESCO National Commissioner. She writes a weekly column in the *Philippine Star*.